3rd edition

Training to Teach in Primary Schools

A practical guide to School-based training and placements

Jane Medwell

 SAGE | LearningMatters

Los Angeles | London | New Delhi
Singapore | Washington DC

Learning Matters
An imprint of SAGE Publications Ltd
1 Oliver's Yard
55 City Road
London EC1Y 1SP

SAGE Publications Inc.
2455 Teller Road
Thousand Oaks, California 91320

SAGE Publications India Pvt Ltd
B 1/I 1 Mohan Cooperative Industrial Area
Mathura Road
New Delhi 110 044

SAGE Publications Asia-Pacific Pte Ltd
3 Church Street
#10–04 Samsung Hub
Singapore 049483

Editor: Amy Thornton
Development editor: Jennifer Clark
Production controller: Chris Marke
Project management: Deer Park Productions
Marketing manager: Lorna Patkai
Cover design: Wendy Scott
Typeset by: C&M Digitals (P) Ltd, Chennai, India
Printed in Great Britain by Henry Ling Limited at
The Dorset Press, Dorchester, DT1 1HD

First published as Successful Teaching Placement:
Primary and Early Years in 2005 by Learning
Matters
Second edition published in 2007
Third edition published in 2015

Library of Congress Control Number: 2014959539

British Library Cataloguing in Publication Data

A catalogue record for this book is available from
the British Library

ISBN 978-1-4739-1307-3
ISBN 978-1-4739-1308-0 (pbk)

At SAGE we take sustainability seriously. Most of our products are printed in the UK using FSC papers and boards. When
we print overseas we ensure sustainable papers are used as measured by the Egmont grading system.
We undertake an annual audit to monitor our sustainability.

Training to Teach
in Primary Schools

SAGE was founded in 1965 by Sara Miller McCune to support the dissemination of usable knowledge by publishing innovative and high-quality research and teaching content. Today, we publish more than 750 journals, including those of more than 300 learned societies, more than 800 new books per year, and a growing range of library products including archives, data, case studies, reports, conference highlights, and video. SAGE remains majority-owned by our founder, and after Sara's lifetime will become owned by a charitable trust that secures our continued independence.

Los Angeles | London | Washington DC | New Delhi | Singapore

Contents

About the author

Jane Medwell

Jane Medwell was a primary teacher before she developed her interest in primary literacy and languages. She taught and did research at the Universities of Wales, Exeter, Plymouth and Warwick before joining the University of Nottingham. Her research interests are primary literacy teaching and learning and the teaching and learning of languages in primary schools. She is currently particularly researching the teaching of handwriting and its relationship with composing, the teaching of primary languages and the use and effects of homework in primary schools.

The author and publishers would like to thank Mary Briggs, Julie Neale, Nigel Palmer and George Raper for their contributions.

Introduction

This book is intended for those who want to teach the Primary phase (5–11) including Key Stages 1 and 2, and those who aim to teach the Early Years (3–8) phase, including Foundation Key Stage and Key Stage 1.

To become a qualified teacher you need to obtain Qualified Teacher Status (QTS) and this is the goal of your Initial Teacher Training (ITT) and induction year. Your Primary or Early Years ITT will take place largely in schools or Early Years settings and you will do school based training in nurseries, primary, junior, infant, first and some middle schools. In this book the term 'schools' covers all these settings and the term 'classroom' is used to encompass all the settings where teaching and learning take place.

Routes to QTS and the role of school based training

All Primary or Early Years teacher training courses leading to QTS include a minimum of 24 weeks in schools and you will work in at least two schools. By the end of an ITT course you should:

- **know and understand the Primary/Early Years curriculum;**
- **be able to plan and prepare for lessons and set pupils' learning objectives;**
- **have strong classroom management skills;**
- **know how to teach pupils with special educational needs and disabilities;**
- **be able to assess pupils effectively.**

When you demonstrate you have achieved this at a level appropriate to a Newly Qualified Teacher (NQT) you will be recommended for the award of Qualified Teacher Status, subject to completion of a successful induction year and you may be awarded a Postgraduate (or Professional) Certificate in Education (PGCE). There are a number of routes you could take to obtain QTS and all are run by a training provider which may be a group of schools, a university or Higher Education Institute (HEI) in partnership with groups of schools, or a charity in partnership with a group of schools. Throughout this book your training provider will be referred to as the Initial Teacher Training Provider (ITT provider). This book helps you to deal with the challenges you will face doing school based training on all of the following routes to QTS.

Each year, most primary trainees undertake graduate, or postgraduate, teacher training which results in either a recommendation of Qualified Teacher Status (QTS), or QTS and an academic award such as PGCE (Postgraduate Certificate in Education or a Professional Graduate Certificate in Education). These are teacher training awards for those who have already completed a degree (or equivalent). These training routes may be led by a university or HEI provider of initial teacher training or by a school-led provider, by a SCITT (school centred initial teacher training) provider, or by a charity such as Teacher First. On school-led routes you will spend most of your time in your base school and learn your subject knowledge and build up your teaching skills gradually. However, school-led and other routes all include blocks of teaching time in other schools. On all ITT routes periods of teaching in more than one school will be assessed towards your QTS.

If you have not already obtained your degree, you may be undertaking an undergraduate degree course that includes QTS. This may be a two-, three- or four-year BA, BSc or BEd. The demands of an undergraduate degree are different from a PGCE because you also have study challenges to address – you are learning to be a successful learner as well as a teacher. However, you will undertake at least 24 weeks in school, most of the time on school placements, and some of these will be assessed towards your QTS.

These are the main routes into Primary (5–11) and Early Years (3–8) teaching but there are a number of other schemes to encourage people into ITT and all involve assessed teaching in schools. This book will be useful to you, whatever your training route, as you seek out the knowledge, understanding and skills you need to be a successful teacher.

MINI CASE MINI CASE **MINI CASE** MINI CASE **MINI CASE** MINI CASE **MINI CASE**

Jane completed her first degree in French and German, travelled abroad for a year, worked for a charity running a play scheme and then began her Primary (5–11) PGCE. She did placements in Years 1 and 3 of a large city school and a longer placement in Year 5 of a suburban school. She has just completed her induction year and hopes to develop foreign language teaching in her junior school. Jane found her PGCE 'a really, really, tough year. But a fantastic experience with an incredible learning curve. I wouldn't have wanted any longer because after my long placement I was desperate to have a class of my own. To move the furniture and so on … '

Zoe had a career as a laboratory technician before her regular visits to her children's school attracted her to school-based work. She became a classroom assistant when her children started full-time school. After three years her head teacher persuaded her to do the teacher training course offered by the teaching school alliance her school belonged to. 'I liked being part time and being in "my" school. At first it was hard to be taken seriously as a teacher when everyone was used to me as an assistant, but my placement in another school really helped me make the transition. I am now an NQT [Newly Qualified Teacher] in the school where I trained and was once a classroom assistant. It's great – I feel real insight into what other staff do and I have learnt so much throughout my training.'

Andrew did a degree in Early Childhood and went straight on to an Early Years PGCE led by a school, in partnership with a local university. His base class was Reception but he did placements in Year 2 and Nursery – in two different schools. 'It was hard to learn the curriculum of both Key Stage 1 and Foundation Key Stage but it was really good to go into three Early Years settings. I feel I have an insight into the whole range and that helps not only the children but also my future promotion. My base class teacher mentored me and gave me the confidence and courage to go for a Reception job.' Andrew is an NQT in a Reception–Nursery unit, working with three teaching assistants.

Petra did a four-year BA with an English specialism. She did short placements in her first and second years in Year 3 and Year 1 in two different schools. In her third and fourth years, Petra had a Year 2 and a Year 6 placement in the same school. 'I started really slowly. I just had no idea what school was like from the teacher's side. But by my third year I was a totally different person. My knowledge of my subjects has changed out of all recognition and I've matured. I have learned so much and grown as a person on my placements and I feel I have grown into the role of the teacher. My mentors and class teachers were tireless in pushing me, but also gave me the confidence I needed.' Petra is now an English co-ordinator in a suburban primary school.

Judy did a degree in biological science and was an environmental health officer for fifteen years. When her children went to secondary school she did a PGCE to re-train as a Primary teacher. 'It was very demanding but I was ready for the challenge and the intensity (one year full time) suited me. I have never regretted it. I found my first placement (in Year 2) awful but then went into Year 5 and loved it. I learnt that each class is very different … .' Judy is an IT co-ordinator in a large city school.

The Teachers' Standards and Qualified Teacher Status (QTS)

The Teachers' Standards (2012), known as 'The Standards', define the minimum level of practice expected of trainees and teachers from the point of being awarded Qualified Teacher Status (QTS). The Teachers' Standards are used to assess all trainees working towards QTS, all those completing their statutory induction period and they are also used to assess the performance of all teachers with QTS. This means that knowing, and understanding, the standards is important to you from the moment you begin your teacher training.

The Teachers' Standards have three parts: the Preamble, Part One and Part Two.

- **The Preamble summarises the values and behaviour that all teachers must demonstrate throughout their careers.**
- **Part One comprises the Standards for Teaching.**
- **Part Two comprises the Standards for Personal and Professional Conduct.**

The eight standards set out in Part One have a number of bulleted subheadings which can be used by trainees and trainers to track progress and assess trainee performance against the standard. The bullet points in the standards are also useful to determine areas where more progress might need to be observed, or to identify areas where a trainee or teacher is already demonstrating excellent practice relevant to that standard.

You need to know The Standards really well, as you will be using them to monitor your progress, set targets and shape your placements. You will have a chance to demonstrate The Standards throughout your school experience but there will be key assessment points where the evidence of your performance will be evaluated against The Standards.

Your course will be designed to enable you to demonstrate you have met these standards but the responsibility for collecting the evidence that you have met them is yours. You will be deeply involved in setting your targets, reviewing evidence and monitoring your progress. Your course handbook or guide will suggest formats and processes for doing this and each course is different. This book refers you to your course guidance whenever necessary.

The role of school based training in ITT

The way each ITT provider plans courses is different, but they involve many similar experiences. As part of your ITT you will probably experience some taught training sessions in a school, training centre or university and may have school teachers from school coming to training centres to teach you. You will almost certainly be asked to audit and improve certain aspects of your subject knowledge through self-study. However, all routes to QTS include school based training (including Nurseries) as a central experience.

In schools you will be able to learn what subject knowledge is important and observe the way the subject knowledge that you are acquiring is used. You will be able to see how teaching techniques are used, how pupils learn and how assessments are made. You will also learn about the culture and values of schools. These experiences are vital to all trainees. In school you will also be able to practise your planning, teaching and assessing, and the use of the subject knowledge you are developing with the support of experienced colleagues. In school you will set targets for yourself and the children and assess and monitor your progress with feedback from at least one member of staff. Your mentor will be able to teach, direct and support you in improving your subject knowledge, planning, teaching and assessing – in short, to train you.

This raises a difficulty with terminology. Each training partnership uses its own terminology and your course may use terms such as 'supervised teaching practice', 'school experience', 'serial days', 'school visits', 'professional placement'. We use the term school based training to include all school based aspects of your training, which may include a number of forms of training:

- **observation of particular children, class or group activities, aspects of management or teachers;**
- **planning lessons and sequences of lessons;**
- **teaching and assessing pupils;**
- **reviewing your progress with feedback from staff;**
- **team teaching;**
- **undertaking directed tasks as part of your course of training;**
- **learning particular policies and curricula;**
- **taking responsibility for the class and pupil performance;**
- **taking part in meetings and in-service sessions;**
- **attending taught sessions in school.**

On some school-led courses, school based training will include most of the time spent in your base class and some shorter periods of training in other schools or classes. For university-led courses, school based training may include a number of periods of training in different schools.

Much, but not all, of your school based training will be based in one class that you will get to know and teach for a substantial period of time. However, you will have some training needs that will require you to observe and teach in other classes or age phases and you will certainly want to develop your knowledge of progression and continuity through the age ranges. School based training is an important part of your preparation to be a teacher and offers training in all aspects of The Standards.

During your school based training you will have a mentor: a person assigned to oversee your training in school and participate in the assessment of your practice, using The Standards. The mentor will have been trained for his/her role and will understand the training route you are taking. Your mentor may, or may not, be the same person as the class teacher who will work with you in your class for all or some of the time you are there, but, either way, your class teacher will also participate in observing, advising and assessing you, as well as offering ongoing support. You may also have a course tutor (known as 'link tutor', 'adviser', 'professional tutor' or 'visiting tutor' in different courses) if you are involved in a course of teacher training. This is the person from the ITT provider (whether it is a university, another school or a representative of a teaching school alliance) who may visit you in school from time to time and offer an 'outsider' view of your performance.

Your training plan

Each person's ITT is unique and each trainee is different because you all have different experiences and different expertise; all training routes try to take this into account. You may have some experience of teaching in, perhaps, English as a Foreign Language (EFL) or a private school, but find the demands of planning unfamiliar curricula challenging. Or you may be very familiar with the curriculum having been, say, a classroom assistant, but find the management demands and performance aspect of teaching a challenge. Each trainee will find some standards easier to address than others. This is why you will have some sort of Individual Training Plan to guide you through your course. This may be called a 'Professional Development Record', a 'training record' or something else. But it will be the document you use to set and monitor your targets. It will contain references to useful aspects of your prior experience as well as what you achieve during your training. Learning to use this sort of plan is important to succeeding in your ITT. It is also an important professional skill because you will have to do this sort of target setting and evidence collection throughout your NQT (Newly Qualified Teacher) year, and the rest of your career. This is explored in Chapter 1.

Short placements

One special type of school based training you may encounter will be the short visit to another educational setting. You may visit a Secondary school to look at the secondary curriculum in action, or to focus on transition to Secondary school. You might visit a Nursery to look at the transition issues involved between the Nursery and Reception classes. You might visit a school with a particularly good teacher of one subject, or good practice in teaching children with English as an Additional Language (EAL) or Special Educational Needs (SEN). If you visit these sessions for a very short period you will not be expected to teach in them but you will usually be given tasks to focus your attention on particular aspects of practice. If you have a chance to teach in these settings, you will need to work closely with the teachers there.

The responsibilities of school based training

All those involved in school based training (mentors, trainees, tutors) take on responsibilities that are discussed in detail later in this book. One type of responsibility raises particular ethical issues – that is, your responsibility to the children in your class. When you are working in a class, you are participating in the education of all the children in that class and they will not get that time, or even that lesson, again. You have a responsibility as a teacher from the moment you begin your ITT. This includes the responsibility to ensure the children are learning as they should. Your class have the right to expect that you know how to behave in school, are well prepared and are able to seek the help and support you need. This book will help you to be well prepared and knowledgeable.

QTS – your driving licence

The achievement of QTS may seem like a distant and demanding goal but remember it is also only a beginning. QTS is rather like a teacher's driving licence. When you achieve the standards for QTS you have achieved your driving licence and are safe to be let loose on a class relatively unsupervised. Like a novice driver, you are not an expert and will continue learning. Indeed, the Teachers' Standards specifically state that ITT providers should assess trainees against The Standards in a way that is consistent with what could reasonably be expected of a trainee teacher prior to the award of QTS, so you will not be expected to teach like an experienced teacher.

Achieving QTS is a big step in your career but only the first step on a long road. It will be followed by a period of induction and further school based training when you are an NQT.

In your ITT, try not to set yourself unreasonable demands. During school based training you will find that you have to juggle demands, do extra research, fill gaps and generally cope with change. This is a normal part of school life and your training. Do not try to demand perfection of yourself and remember that you learn from the less successful experiences as well as the brilliant successes. Do not let off days (and you will have them) get you down.

PRACTICAL TASK PRACTICAL TASK PRACTICAL TASK PRACTICAL TASK PRACTICAL TASK

Before you go further in this book, you should review a number of important documents.

- **Look at your course guidance for your training, which will be available on a website or as a handbook. What school based training takes place in your course and what is expected of you in each block of training, or each placement? Note anything that is unclear to discuss with your mentor or tutor at your next meeting.**

- **Look at your ITT plan. (This may be called a training record, record of professional development, monitoring file, etc.) As soon as you have started your ITT, this plan should contain background information about yourself, your targets and reports. Try to focus on what personal strengths you will be taking into your first placement.**

- **Look at the Teachers' Standards (https://www.gov.uk/government/publications/teachers-standards) and ensure you are familiar with them. Identify any that you are unclear about for discussion with your mentor.**

A SUMMARY OF KEY POINTS

- This book aims to help you to succeed at professional teaching placements in Foundation Key Stage, Key Stage 1 and Key Stage 2.

- If you are undertaking ITT, whatever your training provider, you will be doing school based training.

- Your school based training will involve an ITT provider, mentor, class teacher, and possibly a course tutor.

- Your placements will be guided by your own training plan (or record of professional development).

- As soon as you start your training you assume professional responsibilities and the first of these is to understand your training plan and the Teachers' Standards.

RESOURCES RESOURCES **RESOURCES** RESOURCES RESOURCES **RESOURCES**

The NCTL (National College for Teaching and Learning) is an executive agency of the DfE which seeks to improve the quality of the education workforce and help schools to help each other improve. NCTL works with schools to develop an education system. https://www.gov.uk/government/organisations/national-college-for-teaching-and-leadership

The Department for Education, a government department, is responsible for education and children's services in England. It offers support and advice for those wishing to train as teachers. http://www.education.gov.uk/get-into-teaching

Teacher Training and Education in Wales. Teacher Training in Wales is governed by Welsh legislation and Standards and takes place through three main university based centres for ITT. The GTP (Graduate Teacher Programme) is the school based route offered in Wales. www.teachertraining-wales.org.

1
Managing your school based training

Learning outcomes

This chapter aims to take a long view of your school based training so that you can plan to achieve your goals. By the end of this chapter you should:

- understand the importance of the Teachers' Standards and how to use them to inform your training plan;
- know what activities and review points your training plan may involve;
- know why a training plan is so important;
- understand your central role in managing your training plan.

'A goal without a plan is just a wish'

(Antoine de Saint-Exupery (1900–1944))

The start of your school based training is a good time to consider the path you are about to take, whether you are embarking on a school based programme of Initial Teacher Training (ITT), or at the start of a single placement as part of a longer course. Your long term goals for your ITT are clear:

- **to demonstrate that you have achieved the Teachers' Standards across the key stages you are train-ing to teach, so that you will be recommended for Qualified Teacher Status (QTS);**
- **to get a teaching job so that you can complete your induction period and gain full QTS;**
- **to set out on your Newly Qualified Teacher (NQT) path with clear plans for your future.**

However, the goals alone do not tell you how you are going to achieve them. To understand the steps that will enable you to realise your goals, you need a training plan. This will go through your ITT with you, as you collect evidence of your achievements as a basis for planning your steps towards success.

Your training plan

The broad outline of your training plan is usually a course programme provided by a school, an alliance of schools or a higher education institution (HEI). The course will include these elements.

- **The chance to observe good teachers at work in both of the age phases you are training to teach;**
- **Experience of teaching with a teacher or as part of a teaching team;**
- **Teaching experience in at least two schools;**
- **A gradual build-up of your teaching, planning and assessment responsibilities;**
- **A period where you take responsibility for up to 80 per cent of the class teaching;**

- **Training sessions about key subject knowledge and pedagogic issues;**
- **Chances to audit and improve your subject, curriculum and professional knowledge.**

All of these elements of your training are important, but every trainee tackles them in a different way and it is important that you use them to make the best possible progress. To do this, you must begin your planning with a realistic evaluation of what you can already do.

Understanding your own starting point

It is up to you to ensure that you can take advantage of the experiences which are most useful to you, and ask for specific experiences you need. To identify your training needs you should think carefully about your own knowledge and skills in the following areas:

- **Knowledge of the Primary curriculum and the age phases before and after the two age phases for which you are training;**
- **Knowledge of the subjects you will teach and how the content can be structured;**
- **Knowledge about how children develop and learn;**
- **Interpersonal, presentation and communication skills;**
- **Knowledge of school systems and practices.**

Most courses will help you to evaluate your current knowledge and skills as part of the recruitment process. Others will leave it until the start of your school experience. Reviewing your existing knowledge and skills, and deciding on your starting point for improvement, is a very personal activity and will depend on your previous experience. For example, if you have been working as a TA in a school, you may be familiar with school systems and practices in one school, but still have a long way to go in knowing about a range of schools, or how such systems and practices are developed. If you are studying an undergraduate degree in education you may have done modules about many aspects of the curriculum and feel confident about knowledge of the curriculum, but not how that curriculum is divided up in the school you are training in.

Whatever your previous experience, the success of your school based training is dependent on identification of your strengths and training needs. As a trainee teacher you must be able to discuss your strengths, achievements, learning targets and reflections, with reference to the Teachers' Standards, with your school based mentor. Based on this discussion, you can identify your development targets and the actions you can take to achieve them. This is not a skill which will apply only to your Initial Teacher Training. As you go through your career, you will want to make the best of your annual performance review, which involves discussing your strengths, achievements, weaknesses and targets as a teacher.

MINI CASE MINI CASE **MINI CASE** **MINI CASE** MINI CASE **MINI CASE** **MINI CASE**

starting points

Martin

Martin has just finished his degree and is training in a SCITT partnership. He is in a Y2 base class and has distance learning materials from a university.

(Continued)

(Continued)

The things I am going to teach don't worry me and my initial online audits of English and maths were both very successful. My degree is science based and I know I can research unknown areas of the curriculum. I feel confident about the university training materials and I have a day each week to study them. But my training school has turned out to be very different from the school I volunteered in during my university years. I feel like an imposter and I am worried about acting like a teacher. I need to know the school systems but, more than that, why things work like they do and there seem to be hundreds of things I need to know. I aim to start learning school systems for behaviour management, which is my biggest concern. If I can learn to promote good learning behaviour in Y2, they will see me as a teacher and I can plan useful lessons. My mentor had discussed a starting target of learning the school behaviour management policy, so have read it, observed in three classes and I am using it in my lessons.

Ivana

Ivana has a degree and a masters degree. She has worked as a learning assistant in Year 6 for the last two years.

I am training in the school I have worked in for the last two years and I think this has given me a head start in knowing the school, the children, the parents and teachers. I feel confident in school and know the policies. But the first month of training has been much more different than I expected. I have done audits of my knowledge of the main subjects and I find that there is a lot to work on. I didn't realise just how much I would need to know to plan lessons for Year 5 and, as I was brought up abroad, I think I need to work on some areas people brought up here take for granted. I also did not realise how difficult it is to identify what you want the children to learn. As a TA, I worked from objectives and I hadn't considered where they came from. My first goal is to be able to identify the right objectives, but I know that means I need to know the national curriculum, the school schemes of work, the children in the class and their targets. It is daunting.

Understanding your longer term goal: the Teachers' Standards

The Teachers' Standards set out the key areas that you should be able to demonstrate in your own practice, and you will be assessed against them, so it is important to understand them. The Teachers' Standards are presented in three parts: The Preamble summarises the values and behaviour that teachers must demonstrate throughout their careers; Part One comprises the Standards for Teaching; Part Two comprises the Standards for Personal and Professional Conduct. You will need to demonstrate the values, behaviour and practices for all three.

The standards in Part One are presented as separate headings, each accompanied by a number of bulleted subheadings, which amplify the scope of each heading. These subheadings exist to be used to track progress against the standard, to identify areas where additional development might need to be observed, or to identify areas where a trainee (or teacher) is already demonstrating excellent practice relevant to that standard.

For example, take the standards concerning management of pupil learning behaviour (Part One, Standard 7), which says teachers must:

7. Manage behaviour effectively to ensure a good and safe learning environment

- have clear rules and routines for behaviour in classrooms, and take responsibility for promoting good and courteous behaviour both in classrooms and around the school, in accordance with the school's behaviour policy
- have high expectations of behaviour, and establish a framework for discipline with a range of strategies, using praise, sanctions and rewards consistently and fairly
- manage classes effectively, using approaches which are appropriate to pupils' needs in order to involve and motivate them
- maintain good relationships with pupils, exercise appropriate authority, and act decisively when necessary.

This is a succinct but detailed statement of behaviour management and each of these bullet points will demand sustained teaching and a good deal of evidence. These standards, or even the bullet points, are long-term targets which are too big to be addressed on a single occasion or by a single action. However, they can be broken down into targets and actions which guide you through your training.

MINI CASE MINI CASE MINI CASE **MINI CASE** MINI CASE MINI CASE **MINI CASE**

Martin's first priority was behaviour management.

I started out thinking I needed to 'crack' behaviour management. After a week or so, I decided to focus my efforts a bit and try to do this in the next two weeks. I looked at the standard in the TS which said 'have clear rules and routines for behaviour in classrooms, and take responsibility for promoting good and courteous behaviour both in classrooms and around the school, in accordance with the school's behaviour policy'. So at my mentor meeting I suggested some targets to work towards it:

- *Read the school behaviour policy (on the website);*
- *To find out what acceptable behaviour in all areas of the school is (and unacceptable);*
- *To use the same rewards and sanctions as my class teacher in my maths lesson next week.*

It sounded relatively simple. That week I spent most of my time observing and asking questions. I read the school behaviour policy, observed two teachers during maths to see how they used the rewards and sanctions in the policy; lurked in corridors and the playground to make sure I knew what 'good' behaviour was in the class, the playground and the corridors and listened in on lots of little interactions between teachers and their children, which were frustratingly good natured. When I got to my maths lesson I used the same rules, rewards and sanctions as my class teacher, but my class were still very different when I was teaching them. I just did not have the same confidence as my class teacher, so I asked her about it. She was great and we spent the next four weeks working to make sure that I took the lead in lessons and scanned around the classroom to prevent minor disturbances, rather than reacting to them. The little things like being properly prepared, acting confident, knowing when not to intervene and recognising when an activity was coming to an end, took a long time to understand. Remembering to be 'on task' outside class and see the whole school as my responsibility felt really strange at first. It really took practice, but now I don't even think about it. But it did take a lot of effort to achieve and sustain something which you don't even notice when you start training.

To be a successful teacher you must master the activities in all the bullet points. You will use a target, action, review cycle to focus on different parts of the standards (see Chapter 7) and this will contribute to your training plan.

Assessment against the Teachers' Standards

Your initial teacher training provider (ITTP) will assess you against The Standards in a way that is consistent with what could reasonably be expected of a trainee teacher prior to the award of QTS. You will not be assessed in the same way or against the same expectations as an experienced teacher, but careful scrutiny of the standards, regular review of your training plan and target setting are very important to ensure you make progress. You will aim not only to meet the Teachers' Standards, but to do so at the best possible level. Most training providers grade trainees' teaching at the end of the training period, using grades like outstanding, good or meeting the standards at a minimum level.

To help you to envisage success and plan to achieve it, most providers map the Teachers' Standards, adding descriptions so that you can see what minimum, good and outstanding performance looks like for a trainee on the point of qualification. For example, Table 1.1 shows Part One, Standard 7 set out by UCET and NASBITT (2012) to describe trainee achievement at minimum, good and outstanding levels.

This grid shows you what meeting the standards at a minimum level, a good level and an outstanding level looks like for a trainee teacher. You can use these descriptions to plan your targets throughout your training. Your course may use this grid or a similar set of descriptions to track your growing expertise. It belongs in your training plan for you to regularly reference.

PRACTICAL TASK PRACTICAL TASK **PRACTICAL TASK** PRACTICAL TASK **PRACTICAL TASK**

Review your existing skills and knowledge against the Teachers' Standards

Identify a grid of the Teachers' Standards in your ITT Provider materials or download the UCET/ NASBITT (2012) grid (http://www.ucet.ac.uk/3912). This is a particularly useful format because, as discussed above, you can see what progression in The Standards looks like. Use the highlighter on your computer or highlighter pens to highlight:

- **The parts of The Standards you think you can demonstrate, consistently, as a teacher.**
- **The three parts of The Standards you think are most important for you to develop next.**

These are what you should discuss with your mentor.

Print out this document to take into school with you as part of your training plan (or record of professional development) . It will be very relevant to your early discussions with your mentor and you can update it to identify progress. Make sure you note what evidence you have for each standard and where you have filed it.

Your training plan

Your personal training plan will be based on your initial review of your knowledge and skills with achievement of the Teachers' Standards as your goal. However, you will start with only a broad outline of your training plan based on the structure of your training

Table 1.1 Teachers' Standards, Part One, Standard 7

	By the end of the programme of ITE, all those trainees recommended for the award of QTS will have demonstrated that:	Those trainees rated as 'good' at the end of the programme of ITE may have demonstrated that:	Those trainees rated as 'outstanding' at the end of the programme of ITE may have demonstrated that:
7 Manage behaviour effectively to ensure a good and safe learning environment -have clear rules and routines for behaviour in classrooms, and take responsibility for promoting good and courteous behaviour both in classrooms and around the school, in accordance with the school's behaviour policy -have high expectations of behaviour, and establish a framework for discipline with a range of strategies, using praise, sanctions and rewards consistently and fairly -manage classes effectively, using approaches which are appropriate to pupils' needs in order to involve and motivate them -maintain good relationships with pupils, exercise appropriate authority, and act decisively when necessary.	They work within the school's framework for behaviour and can apply rules and routines consistently and fairly. They have high expectations and are aware of the range of strategies that experienced teachers use to promote positive behaviour. They are able to apply these appropriately, in the context of the schools policy using sanctions and rewards, including praise, in order to create an environment supportive of learning. They understand when to seek additional support in addressing the needs of pupils where significantly challenging behaviour is demonstrated. They recognise that planning appropriate lessons which challenge learners, teaching using a variety of strategies which address pupils' needs and employing appropriate assessment strategies will all contribute to successful behaviour management. They show understanding of how barriers to learning can impact on pupil behaviour and have begun to apply strategies to address these, working alongside experienced teachers and support staff as appropriate. They understand that behaviour management is context-dependent and are able to articulate which factors may contribute to more challenging behaviour being exhibited within their classes.	They work within the school's framework for behaviour and apply rules and routines consistently and fairly. They consistently have high expectations and understand a range of strategies that experienced teachers use to promote positive behaviour and apply these effectively, including use of school sanctions and rewards and use of praise, in order to create an environment supportive of learning. They manage behaviour effectively so that learners demonstrate positive attitudes towards the teacher, their learning and each other allowing lessons to flow smoothly so that disruption is unusual. They actively seek additional support in addressing the needs of pupils where significantly challenging behaviour is demonstrated.	They rapidly adapt to the different circumstances in which they train, working confidently within the frameworks established in different settings and applying rules and routines consistently and fairly. They consistently have high expectations and understand a range of strategies that experienced teachers use to promote positive behaviour and apply these very effectively, including use of school sanctions and rewards and use of praise, in order to create an environment highly supportive of learning. They manage pupil behaviour with ease so that learners display very high levels of engagement, courtesy, collaboration and cooperation. They actively seek additional support in addressing the needs of pupils where significantly challenging behaviour is demonstrated.

(Part 1, Standard 2. Taken from UCET/NASBITT, 2012, http://www.ucet.ac.uk/3912)

course, which specifies when and what age groups you will teach. You must demonstrate that you can address the standards across the two age phases for which you are training to teach and, although you may spend much longer in one age phase than the other, you must still be able to teach successfully in both age phases.

The example of Keisha's course (see Table 1.2) shows you the training opportunities in a SCITT course, which involved a university. The review column shows when Keisha reviewed her progress against all the standards, and also how she used her mentor meetings. Her preparation for teaching began when she applied for a training place.

Table 1.2 Keisha's training opportunities

Pre-course experience

	Course provision	Activities	Review points
May	Interview in a partnership school and offer of a place.	Complete skills tests. Complete online audits of English, maths and science subject knowledge.	Identify knowledge of science processes and grammar to study before next term.
July	Two weeks spent in Y4 in Keisha's 'home' school with one other trainee. Works in her 'base class' and others.	Keisha meets her mentor, her class teacher and next year's children, looks at the school scheme of work for Year 4.	Complete and share her initial review against the standards with the mentor.

Term 1

	Course provision	Activities	Review points
Sept-Oct 14	School induction and teaching lessons. Weekly mentor meetings. Fridays – training at the university (English, maths, science, child protection, etc.).	Keisha observes in each year group. She teaches English and maths from her teacher's plans.	Use weekly mentor meetings to focus on lesson planning, teaching and evaluation. Reviews school policies on the school network.
14 Oct-End Nov	Six-week teaching experience in her base class (Y4), five days a week with weekly mentor observations and feedback.	Keisha builds up her planning, teaching and marking in English, maths and science to 50% timetable.	Weekly mentor meetings used to review Keisha's teaching file, including lesson plans and observation feedback.
Dec	Four days per week in base class (Y4). Fridays in university. Weekly mentor meetings.	Team teaching with class teacher.	Keisha uses her teaching file and observations to review her progress against The Standards grid and shares it with her mentor. Mentor completes a report about the six-week teaching experience block, using The Standards grid to highlight progress and set development targets for next term.

Term 2

Jan –Feb 7	Teaching in base class with teacher. Fridays in university focusing on foundation subjects, assessment etc.	Keisha teaches in her 'home class', taking responsibility for planning sequences of lessons and building her experience of assessment and recording pupil progress.	Weekly mentor meetings focus on targets identified at the end of last term.
February 7–15	Preparatory visit to KS1 school	Keisha spends 5 days at School 2, a member of her SCITT partnership, observing and teaching parts of lessons	Meets with School 2 mentor to discuss teaching experience. Revises phonics.
February and March	Five weeks teaching experience in Year 1 of School 2. Weekly meetings with Mentor 2.	Keisha builds up her teaching to 60%. She plans, teaches and assesses across the curriculum and does all the phonics for the last two weeks.	Weekly mentor meetings used to review Keisha's teaching file, including lesson plans and observation feedback. Keisha uses her teaching file and observations to review her progress against The Standards grid and shares it with her mentor. Mentor completes a report about the six-week teaching experience block, using The Standards grid to highlight progress and set development targets for her last term.

Term 3

April	Four days per week in home school with mentor observations. Fridays in other schools in the partnership doing training.	Keisha teaches in her 'home class' across the curriculum building her experience of assessment and recording pupil progress.	Weekly mentor meetings focus on targets identified in the last report of progress against the standards and as a result of observation feedback.
May 7– end June	Sustained teaching experience. Weekly observations from mentor, head teacher and subject co-ordinators. Days out to observe SAT processes. Keisha applies for and accepts a post a partner school for next year.	Keisha builds up her teaching timetable to 80% and focuses on pupil progress in her home class.	Weekly mentor meetings used to review Keisha's teaching file, including observation feedback and focus on pupil progress.
July	Team teaching with class teacher	Keisha and her class teacher conduct final pupil assessments, sports day, class assembly. Keisha visits her NQT school for a week to meet her new colleagues and class.	Keisha reviews her progress against The Standards grid and shares it with her mentor. Mentor completes a final report, including targets for the NQT year.

This example shows the planned training experiences Keisha did, in her home school and another school in the partnership. She did some training days in a university and also whole school training as part of staff meetings, non-pupil days and days organised by her SCITT in a variety of schools. In addition to these training opportunities, she observed other teachers, got feedback on her teaching and did a formal review of her progress each term. All her training experiences were recorded in her training plan file.

Her reviews against The Standards were kept together in her training plan file (often called a record of professional development or professional development plan) with records of where the evidence she had collected for each standard could be found. This was a one year course, so if you are a part time trainee or doing a longer course, you would expect this sort of activity to be spread over a longer period of time.

This example shows the 'big picture' of school experience, but the little steps are important in your growth as a teacher. The Teachers' Standards are a set of long-term targets. The actions to address them are all the planned school based training that is part of your course. However, you will not achieve The Standards by sitting back and waiting for someone to tell you what to do. To make progress you must break down those big targets into more manageable targets and use a cycle of target setting, action and review to make the most of the opportunities in your school based training. This is discussed in more detail in Chapter 7 of this book.

Target setting during your school based training

Throughout your school based training (and each year in your teaching career) you will be expected to identify and address clear targets to help you improve your performance towards all aspects of the Teachers' Standards and identify actions which will enable you to meet those targets. You will have the support of your mentor to do this.

Your mentor or tutors will help you to set initial targets based on general expectations. Targets set further on in your training, such as those in Keisha's second or third term, will be based on a review of earlier school based training. With your mentor or your course tutor, you will discuss your mentor's report from the previous period of school based training, your observation notes, your teaching file and your own self-evaluation to identify your progress and needs.

Your progress is likely to be better if you identify specific actions that will enable you to achieve your targets. A target such as :'To learn the SEND policy, class SEND needs and support for children in my class' is perfectly reasonable, if it is accompanied by actions such as: 'Read the SEND policy; meet with the SENCO to review provision of the children with SEN in my class'. When you have done this, you can review those targets and set more.

When you set medium-term targets for a term or placement you can expect that some of them will be ticked off and replaced with new targets during the placement. Others will last for the duration of the term and be more fully reviewed at the end of the term or period in school, ready for your next period of school based training.

Evidence to demonstrate you are meeting the Teachers' Standards

As a trainee teacher, you aim to collect the evidence necessary to demonstrate you have met The Standards, across the whole period of your training, which might include:

- **Records of observations of your teaching across the age range you are training for, from mentors, head teacher, tutor or class teacher observations;**
- **Lesson plans and sequences of lesson plans, with evaluations;**
- **Assessments and records of children's work, showing your marking and recording of progress;**
- **Reports (sometimes called profiles) written about your teaching, normally termly, throughout your training and which evaluate your performance against the Teachers' Standards;**
- **Files and professional records you are keeping which demonstrate your professional standards and practices.**

All these sources of evidence will contribute to assessments of your teaching against the Teachers' Standards and it is up to you to collect them and discuss them with your mentor to inform his/her judgements about your performance. Most mentors will expect you to review The Standards and evaluate your performance before discussing it with the mentor. In the example above, Keisha recorded on the grid where she had found the evidence for each part of the standard. Some courses will ask you to collect it all together in a single file.

Although the mentor's assessment will be informed by his/her experience of levels of performance appropriate to NQTs, the evidence you share will inform these assessments and will certainly include information which mentors have not seen or do not remember.

MINI CASE MINI CASE MINI CASE **MINI CASE** MINI CASE MINI CASE **MINI CASE**

Martin did most of his teaching in Year 2, but also had a Year 5 placement in another school in the alliance.

In my base class I worked steadily to learn to manage Y2 behaviour well. Each week I chose targets which took me towards that Standard 7 'Manage behaviour effectively to ensure a good and safe learning environment'. But when I went into my second school, I found that particular standard incredibly tough with Y5. I read the policy, observed other teachers, and used the same strategies as them – strategies which I had worked hard at, in Y2! But the class was still noisy and distracted. It was really hard work. Two weeks in, after a really bumpy lesson, I sat down with my mentor to review a lesson observation. I went through all the things I'd done to learn about behaviour management. He said I was using good strategies, but the work just wasn't quite right for the children so they were losing focus. So my targets were about assessing the children's progress, setting objectives and pace, which didn't feel right. But it made a big difference and, once the work was better matched to the class, I could make lessons more fun. In the end, they were a really good class. All these aspects of teaching are linked and, just when you think you have got one part of teaching right, you have to look at the whole picture all over again. I will be serious about getting the work right for my NQT class.

Key personal qualities to take you through your training

This chapter has focused on the ways you can plan, manage and reflect on your school based training. This demands certain personal qualities, including openness, reflectiveness and resilience.

Openness

As a trainee teacher you need to be open to comment and criticism about your teaching; teaching is no longer a private activity between teacher and pupils. Your colleagues, including teachers, fellow trainees, teaching assistants, mentors and tutors, will share their views about your teaching, especially if you ask them to! To get the very most from feedback, whether it is day-to-day comments or detailed lesson observation notes, requires you to be open to it. When a colleague comments about your teaching, thank them and make sure you know what they mean. Ask them to explain and give examples so you can think about what they are saying. Try to avoid speaking (or thinking) defensively. Instead, ask yourself whether you can learn from this. The most important thing to remember is that the people involved in your training want you to be as successful as possible.

Reflectiveness

You will almost certainly think about your teaching and talk to colleagues about it too. You might think or tell someone that 'My lesson went well' or 'My pupils didn't seem to understand' or 'My students were badly behaved today'. However, without more time spent focusing on the details of a lesson or discussing what has happened, you might not be able to identify what has happened and why. Reflective teaching is a more systematic process of collecting, recording and analysing thoughts and observations of pupil learning, and then going on to making changes. You should evaluate all your lessons in terms of pupil learning and your teaching. It can be very useful to have another view on this, from your teacher, mentor or other observer. However, to get the most from the views of others, you must be open to listen to them, without getting defensive. It is very unlikely that everything said to you about your teaching will be praise, so you must practise accepting, listening to and acting on the advice of others.

Resilience

The emotional demands of teaching are huge and well-recognised. Teachers were one of the first professional groups in the UK to have government-sponsored guidance about how to prevent and manage stress. However, demonstrating resilience by being able to recover from everyday, as well as especially challenging, difficulties is important for your survival and happiness in your work. Research in this area shows that although some teachers do suffer stress as a result of the demands of their job, others do not (Day and Gu, 2010) and that a focus on resilience might be more productive than a focus on stress.

Resilience appears for beginning teachers as they develop confidence that they will succeed in their efforts to get Qualified Teacher Status. If you feel that you have a sense of agency in your role as teacher you will be more resilient and be able to weather the ups and downs of school based training. It is really important that you recognise that resilience is not an innate psychological quality, but a capacity which is socially constructed and recognises that learning to teach is complex, demanding and teaching is an interactive profession.

You should work with your mentor and colleagues to:

- **establish realistic expectations of roles and responsibilities for yourself and your mentor;**
- **devise challenging targets for development but also make sure you recognise success;**
- **recognise the challenges in learning to teach and the reasons for these, and establish a collaborative rather than individualistic approach to seeking solutions;**
- **establish mutually respectful relationships which challenge and support;**
- **critique your own beliefs, values and practice;**
- **work with your colleagues to improve teaching and learning for your children;**
- **develop a supportive, trusting network of peers and colleagues who work collaboratively and appreciate their role in others' development (thereby exercising reciprocity).**

(Smethem and Hood, 2011)

REFLECTIVE TASK

Being resilient will enable you to make the most of your opportunities for learning during your training and deal with the pressures of teaching, learning and taking advice.

Try one of the online resilience scales, such as http://www.resiliencescale.com/papers/resilience_core.html

These scales use similar questions to help you reflect on your ability to bounce back and learn from experience.

Ask yourself:

- **What aspects of school life are most stressful for me?**
- **How can I deal with these situations so that I do not feel pressured and can learn from them?**

A SUMMARY OF KEY POINTS

- Whatever the course of training you have chosen, school based training is central to it.
- Your course offers a whole range of school based training opportunities. Some will be more important for you than others.
- You are responsible for making the most of your school based training opportunities by evaluating your needs, setting targets and taking action.
- The Teachers' Standards are your long-term goal, but to achieve them you need to plan specific targets and actions that will get you there.
- The Teachers' Standards can be addressed at a minimum level, a good level or an outstanding level. You want to do as well as possible. This means tracking your progress.
- As you go through your ITT you will compile a training plan (or record of professional development). This will include your achievements and targets.

(Continued)

(Continued)

- Your mentor, class teacher and course tutor will help you build your teaching experience and participate in your assessment. Make sure they have evidence of your achievements and can easily look at your training plan.

- To succeed in teaching and teacher training, reflectiveness and resilience are key qualities. You can develop these.

RESOURCES RESOURCES **RESOURCES** RESOURCES RESOURCES **RESOURCES**

Day, C. and Gu, Q. (2010) *The New Lives of Teachers*. London: Routledge.

Smethem, L. and Hood, P. (2011) 'Fostering resilience through initial teacher education', in Day, D. Edwards, A., Griffiths, A., and Gu, Q. *Key Messages from an ESRC Seminar Series*, Nottingham: University of Nottingham.

2
Preparing for school based teacher training

Learning outcomes

This chapter aims to make you aware of how your school based training experiences are organised, what is expected of you and what you can expect of those involved in your training. The chapter is focused on helping you to prepare for a setting that is new to you.

By the end of this chapter you should:

- **know how and why school based training settings and placements are selected;**
- **be able to research your school;**
- **be able to draft an email or letter to your school;**
- **know who will be closely involved in your training;**
- **be able to prepare a teaching file;**
- **be able to join a teaching union.**

Selecting settings for school based training

Some ITT routes will recruit you directly to the school where you will do much of your training, but most partnerships will have a wide range of schools to choose from. All training partnerships running ITT will ensure you have experience in more than one school. This ensures you are prepared to teach in schools generally, rather than in just one particular school. It also offers you a much wider range of staff, children and resources to learn from. You may do most of your experience in a home school and shorter placements in other schools, or do a number of placements in different schools during an undergraduate training programme.

Here are some of the most frequently asked questions on this subject.

Frequently asked questions

1. 'How will my school based training settings be selected?'

If you are training in a large partnership or university-led programme, your ITT provider will assign places in the training partnership school on the basis of the information it has been given by you and by the school. So, if you are asked to fill in a form with personal details and questions about travel and domestic arrangements, make sure you are specific. ITT providers will accommodate you as conveniently as possible, taking into account the following factors:

- **your training needs (the age phase or school type you need, any specific targets you have to address during this placement);**
- **the range of school based training placement offers from schools in the partnership;**
- **the number of trainees who need to be accommodated;**
- **the geography and your travel arrangements;**
- **the training history of the school (you will not be placed in a school with a poor record of training or a school that has just gone into special measures);**
- **your commitments (if you are part time, not all placements will be suitable).**

School based teacher training carries the same professional demands as other jobs. You may have to make domestic arrangements to ensure you can meet those commitments. It is not reasonable to expect placements to be arranged around pet care unless you are doing a part-time course. Smaller partnerships, which involve only a few schools, may also want to take into account the need to swap trainees so that the arrangement is suitable for all schools.

2. 'Aren't all schools the same for the purposes of school based training?'

Schools decide very carefully when they can best train trainees and the classes trainees can be placed in. Schools make offers based on that information and only offer to take a trainee when it will work for all those involved, including the children. These offers are always provisional, because schools are dynamic, changing places. A school may have a change of staff or particular year group that means they cannot take the trainees they had planned for.

3. 'There is a really convenient school at the end of my road. Why can't I just go there?'

All schools offering school based training or placements have to be part of the training partnership you are being trained in. If you are training in a small SCITT provider, this may involve only two or three schools and if you are training in a university partnership it may involve several hundred schools. However, each of these schools will share the same expectations of you, make similar demands and have staff trained to support you in particular ways. The convenient school you mention may not be in the training partnership.

Alternatively, the school you mention may be in the partnership, but may want to work with trainees at a different time, not want a trainee at all this year or already have a trainee.

4. 'Why isn't the school at the end of my road in the training partnership?'

It is up to schools whether they join a training partnership. Most schools do, but this does not mean they can support placements every year. They may have a large number of NQTs or have school priorities that mean they cannot offer placements in one particular year. The school you mention may even belong to a different training partnership. Some schools are not in training partnerships. They may have school issues that mean they cannot participate, such as serious weaknesses they are addressing.

5. 'Can I choose my own school?'

Although some SCITT partnerships may recruit you directly to your base school, most partnerships will recruit trainees and negotiate their settings within the partnership. This means you usually cannot choose. Your training school needs to be in the training partnership for the reasons discussed above. You are training to teach in all types of schools in your age phase, not just those you like. Your school must be chosen with a range of factors in mind and your training needs are the most important. This usually means you cannot choose. The only exception is where you do a SCITT scheme in a particular school but even then you will be assigned to classes in your base school and to another school with your training needs and other factors or priorities. Do not approach schools yourself unless you are asked to do so – you may cause real professional offence.

6. **'I am doing a PGCE in a large partnership and I have been assigned a school at some distance. My friend is in a school much nearer my home. Can we swap?'**

Check with the person who manages the training in your partnership. It may be possible to swap. But it may not, for good reasons. Either you or your friend may have training needs that dictate your placement in those schools. It may be that those schools can offer different age phases, or examples of particularly good practice. It may be that the travel arrangements of several trainees can be accommodated using this placement pattern. If the schools already know who to expect, changing places will cause inconvenience.

7. **'For my other key stage experience, I will be doing five weeks in a school that has much more challenging behaviour than my base school. Can I refuse this offer?'**

You are training to be a teacher who can teach in all Primary (or Early Years) schools. If this school is satisfactory in OFSTED terms and is part of the training partnership then it is probably a good training setting and you should take advantage of the training it offers. Remember, too, that a school in a challenging area may actually be very successful indeed and may offer you some excellent models of good practice. In this case you will have the chance to see successful behaviour policies in action and work with teachers who are used to this challenging setting – learn from the support they can give you.

PRACTICAL TASK PRACTICAL TASK **PRACTICAL TASK** PRACTICAL TASK **PRACTICAL TASK**

When you know which school you will be doing your school based training in, either as a base school or a placement school, there are some things you should do before you visit it. If you have been recruited by a school-led partnership, you should already have found out some information about the partnership.

Use the internet to find out as much as you can about the school:

- **Search the OFSTED site for the school's most recent OFSTED report.**
- **How old is the OFSTED report? Does this mean some things will have changed, or that another OFSTED inspection is due?**
- **What weaknesses did OFSTED identify? These may well be areas the school will be working on and may particularly benefit you.**
- **Find out whether the school has a website and see what it tells you about the school. You might also check www.ukschoolguide.com – a website directory of all schools based in the UK.**

(Continued)

(Continued)

- **How large is the school? Does it have Key Stage 1 and Key Stage 2 and a Nursery? If you are aiming to look at transition between key stages this may offer you particular opportunities.**
- **What are the school's strengths? Some of these may be of particular interest to you.**
- **Does the school undertake particular events like residential trips that might affect you?**

Check the location and your travel arrangements for the school

If you are travelling to school by public transport, make the journey at the appropriate time of day before your start date. You can then make sure you allow enough time on the day itself. If you will be driving to school, the same applies – check how long the journey actually takes: maps can be deceptive. When you know what your journey will be like you can make any domestic arrangements you need.

Explore the area around the school

When you get to the school take the time to explore the streets around it, ensuring that you choose a safe time to do so. Take a good look round so you can form some impressions about the lives of the children you will be teaching. You will also be able to identify what resources children will have experienced (such as shops, cafes, etc.) and what local features might be a part of your teaching (park, mosque, church, village hall, etc.).

Introduce yourself

When you know the name of your mentor (and head teacher) you may be advised to write to the school introducing yourself. Send your letter to the head teacher and the school mentor, to ensure it gets to the correct person but make sure that you get the head teacher's and mentor's names right.

Schools increasingly communicate using email and if you have been given your mentor's email, you can use this. If you have not got a specific email for the mentor it is best to write a letter first, in case your school or mentor does not use email routinely. You can always use the school's published email address to enquire for the head's and mentor's professional email addresses but do so well in advance and, if you do not get them, send a letter.

When you offer your contact details do provide as many as possible, but be aware that if you offer an email address you must check it daily. As a trainee teacher you should be thoughtful about your email address and not give your personal address if it is inappropriate. You will be given a school or university email address by your partnership to use for professional emails – but not for personal activities like shopping. You must check this email address regularly.

Your email or letter should not be too long. We recommend less than one side of A4 and definitely less than two. Make sure you keep a copy to put in your training plan or record of professional development.

Include:

- **your name, contact address, telephone number and email;**
- **degree subject and subject interests if you are a graduate or your A level subjects (or access) and subject focus if you are an undergraduate;**
- **your educational achievements;**
- **previous experience with children, including placements undertaken so far;**

- **work experience and particular skills gained from it;**
- **personal skills (such as music, computing, sports);**
- **anything you think you could contribute to the school;**
- **what you would particularly like to achieve from this placement.**

Sample letter

Norma Smith

3, Chapel Hill,

Coundon,

Newcastle

NE21 5BQ

Mrs Hughes

School Mentor

Manor Park School

Littleton Road

Newcastle

Dear Mrs Hughes,

I am writing to introduce myself before I meet you on 4 March on my first PGCE placement day.

I started the PGCE in Primary Education in September as a mature student and I have had a range of experience that I hope will be useful to me in becoming a teacher. After doing my degree in maths at Reading University, I worked for ten years as an accountant, mainly doing audits, before having my own children. My children's education introduced me to the world of children and I worked as a play assistant in a Nursery group and, for two years, as a classroom assistant in a Primary school.

On the PGCE course so far we have concentrated on the demands of teaching English, mathematics and science and I have been teaching these subjects in a Y5 class at The Larches Primary School. My first profile report was good and I have targets to work on teaching science. I hope I will be able to do some of this when I teach in your Y2 class. I am also very keen to learn about KS1 assessment. I will bring my record of training with me on my serial days and I look forward to setting first placement targets during those days.

I will be coming to school on 4 October for the first of the three serial placement days. I will arrive at around 8.15 and I hope I will be able to meet you then. If this is not an appropriate time perhaps you could let me know.

Yours sincerely

Norma Smith

(Continued)

(Continued)

Sample email

Dear Mrs Grey,

I am writing to introduce myself as your SCITT trainee. We met very briefly at the recruitment day and I am looking forward to meeting you again on 3 September.

I am thrilled to be training as a teacher with the Rectory SCITT partnership and look forward to getting to know Oakdene School. I have had a range of experience that I hope will be useful to me in becoming a teacher. After doing my degree in history at Sheffield University, I worked overseas, teaching English, mostly in Asia, before returning to the UK to get married and have my own children. As they became more independent I began to volunteer in their school and, more recently, I was employed as a classroom assistant in Year 4, working specifically with a child with special needs. I found this role challenging and exciting and I think it has taught me a good deal about the importance of individualising teaching. I was very pleased to be accepted on the SCITT course and I have used the audit materials for English, maths and science. During the summer I worked hard to improve my subject knowledge, particularly in maths.

I will be coming to school on 3 September for the pre-term training day. I will arrive at around 8.15 a.m. and I hope I will be able to meet you then. If this is not an appropriate time perhaps you could let me know.

Sincerely

Elizabeth Green

Join a union

Join at least one of the main teaching unions (we recommend joining all of them). All offer free membership to trainees and this includes valuable insurance and advice about all sorts of professional matters. Joining a union is discussed more fully on page 36.

What to expect on your professional placement

When a school has accepted you for school based training, or even for a shorter placement, it has a commitment to ITT and is looking forward to training you during your placement. The training partnership will have a contract with the school that sets out what they can expect of you and what you can expect of the school. Look at your training programme or guidance where you will find this is set out for you. Each training partnership is different, so check your details carefully.

What to expect of your school

Some schools will be part of a SCITT partnership based around a teaching school alliance, academy chain or another cluster of schools. Others will be in partnerships of schools and universities. Some schools will work directly with universities to offer placements. The nature of your partnership affects who you will work with, but on any school based training you will trained by and assessed by the school staff and school mentor. Other tutors from the university, or other schools, will occasionally come out to check arrangements and moderate assessments.

MINI CASE MINI CASE **MINI CASE** **MINI CASE** MINI CASE **MINI CASE** **MINI CASE**

Maureen was a SCITT trainee based in a school in Coventry. Her school was in a SCITT partnership based around a teaching school alliance.

During my ITT training I did teaching experiences in two classes in my base school and also a long teaching experience in another school in our teaching school alliance. During my training the school mentor met me fortnightly to discuss my progress, set and review targets and plan the training experiences I needed. I usually planned the agenda of those meetings and took the notes, but not always – we negotiated. These meetings were the backbone of my training and I continued them with the mentor in my final school, in a slightly different format.

I also had weekly observations during teaching experience, with written feedback, mostly done by the school mentor and the class teachers of my classes. I also had observations and feedback from subject co-ordinators in the school, just as other teachers in the school did.

As a result of the observations and feedback I got, I was able to take action to improve my subject knowledge and teaching. I used these observations and discussions to pinpoint what I needed to look up or what training course would benefit me. Sometimes very simple actions, such as reading school policies or discussions with other members of staff, brought significant training benefits for me – but some of these had to be identified in discussion. I'm not convinced I'd have thought of them on my own.

I was observed once by another mentor from the partnership in both my early placements and an external moderator from the teaching school alliance came and observed me on my last teaching experience. Although it was a bit stressful, I found this reassuring and I was pleased that someone outside my immediate school was checking that my performance was comparable to others in my position.

My school mentor filled out my profiles (the assessment summaries done each term for each of my teaching experiences) and wrote the reports. I had to include these with my evidence file to get recommended for QTS.

Ruth was a final year undergraduate trainee in a large Primary school in Leamington Spa. Her school was in a full partnership.

I did my third year placement in two classes in the school (Years 1 and 2) and a fourth year placement in the Year 4 class. I had weekly meetings with my mentor at 2 pm every Friday. At these meetings we would look at three main things. Firstly, the observation and feedback from the observation that week, if there was one. Next we looked briefly at my targets for the placement and finally, we checked The Standards to see which ones to prioritise for the next few weeks. In this way we always had a number of targets we could discuss. At our meetings I often came with questions I'd collected through the week because my mentor was not always accessible during the week and I didn't like to keep asking the other staff. I found I needed to write them down.

The mentor and class teacher did observations, mostly. The head teacher did observe me once and an Ofsted inspector did too. It was nerve wracking but I felt I was more prepared than the other teachers because I was so used to having my teaching observed and commented upon. Sometimes we

(Continued)

(Continued)

discussed the notes straight after the lesson but it wasn't always possible. Sometimes we had a quick talk after school.

My university tutor came and observed once in each class on first placement and twice in the final placement. This was useful for me because I felt I got an objective view.

My mentor did my placement reports. These go into my record of professional development (training plan) as well as to the university and show that I was successful in the placement.

Arshun was a SCITT trainee in a very small school near Plymouth. His school was in partnership with a group of schools and a university and so he had more attention from his university tutor.

I basically saw my mentor all the time because I was in her class. She was a teaching head and I worked in her class with her and with the other teacher who shared the class. We planned meetings every week but, realistically, I think we met about once a fortnight (school activity permitting) which was plenty. She was very organised and had a focus for each meeting. Usually, this was an observation done of my teaching, the pupils' progress and tracking or a particular aspect of teaching she wanted to draw to my attention, such as planning from the rolling programme or behaviour management. On a couple of occasions we scrapped the agenda just to talk about behaviour management because I was preoccupied by it then. I also had a specific meeting about a task the university had set me during this term.

I was formally observed, with written notes and lesson plans, by the other teacher in the class three times in the five weeks I was in the school. I also had one observation from the university tutor who discussed it with me and helped me to identify points to improve and things I should do to help me keep developing. It was helpful to have their insights and my tutor identified things I hadn't thought of.

When it came to assessment, the mentor wrote a report which she discussed with the tutor. They talked to each other and to me in preparing these and there weren't any surprises.

What to expect of your school mentor

The Teachers' Standards emphasise that you must 'develop effective professional relationships with colleagues, knowing how and when to draw on advice and specialist support' and 'take responsibility for improving teaching through appropriate professional development, responding to advice and feedback from colleagues' (Teachers' Standard 8). This standard involves a combination of personal responsibility for your professional development, good communication with colleagues and the ability to act on advice. This is the basis of a mentoring relationship that will be your chief vehicle of learning through professional placement. The school mentor will be a teacher who has undertaken training and takes a lead role in dealing with trainees in the school. Your mentor is crucial to your training on professional placement. In some schools your mentor may also be your class teacher, but often the mentor is a senior member of staff who can provide the sort of objective support that we all need from time to time. The role of the school mentor will vary depending on the type of partnership the school is engaged in, but in general you can expect the following.

Your mentor will:

- **be your main point of contact with the school;**
- **know the school well, including the strengths of different members of staff, resources and opportunities;**

- meet you on a regular basis to help you to set targets, evaluate progress, and identify experiences you want to have;
- know the Teachers' Standards and how to help you demonstrate them;
- provide a link with the university or lead school, if one is involved in your training course;
- be aware of your workload and help you to plan it effectively so that you can meet your training needs;
- observe some of your teaching and give feedback;
- assess and report on your progress. The mentor is usually responsible for assessing you towards the end of the placement and filling out a full report or profile of your progress against the standards so far. In some partnerships the mentor may do this in conjunction with a tutor from a university or college;
- be trained, know what to expect of trainees and pass information about trainees to other members of staff.

These roles are discussed more fully in Chapter 6.

Contacts

Your mentor will know the dates and expectations of your school based training before you arrive. If you are doing a placement outside your base school, he or she may also have seen previous reports about your teaching or assessments of progress against The Standards so far and will have limited knowledge about you.

The mentor will also have a guidance for the specific phase of your school based training or placement. However, it is a good idea to discuss the school based training requirements clearly at the beginning of your time in the school. Mentors can help you to complete school-based tasks you may have or work you have to do for an assignment. Although they will know about these in advance you must discuss them with your mentor and plan when to complete them.

In school your mentor is the person who can provide details of the school policies, staff, etc. (see Chapter 6). Your mentor can also arrange training experiences you might need: perhaps observing a particular teacher who is good at something you are trying to get to grips with, or arranging a demonstration or discussion with an IT co-ordinator. If there is something you particularly need to be involved in, such as National Tests or report writing, you should always discuss it with the mentor, who will help you to make arrangements.

On your first day you should arrange to meet your mentor before school.

Planning, teaching assessment and recording

Your mentor will agree a timetable with you. This is not quite as specific as it sounds because of your developing needs and the pace of school life. At first your timetable will involve a great deal of observation. As you learn more about the class the amount of teaching will increase.

Your mentor will routinely plan for your involvement in the teaching of English, maths and science. Where you have targets that involve other subjects you will need to discuss these with your mentor and class teacher to ensure that, if they are not being taught in your class this term, you can go to another class.

Observation of your teaching

Mentors will manage and participate in observation of your teaching but they may not do it all themselves. Class teachers and subject co-ordinators may observe you teaching sessions and give you written and verbal feedback. Discuss who will observe you and when.

Regular review meetings

Your mentor will meet regularly with you to discuss:

- **observations and feedback;**
- **the children's progress;**
- **your performance against your targets;**
- **setting more specific targets;**
- **your school based tasks (if you have any);**
- **your performance against the Teachers' Standards.**

Assessment

As your school based training or placement progresses your mentor will usually take the lead in writing a report about your progress. Different courses give these reports different names (profiles, reports, assessments, etc.). This report will be linked to the Teachers' Standards and will contain judgements about the strengths and weaknesses of your teaching and subject knowledge based on the evidence provided by observation feedback sheets, mentor meetings, discussion, observations by other staff and the contents of your files. There may be an interim report about halfway through the term or placement. The report will be read by you, the mentor and any course staff involved in your training and will be the basis of target-setting for subsequent placement, further course-based work or for your NQT year.

What to expect of the class teacher

Throughout your school based training the class teacher will provide most of your day-to-day support. At the beginning of any placement, you will be observing your class teacher very closely to see how he or she works with the children, what the rules and expectations of classroom behaviour are and how your teacher rewards and enforces these expectations. Your first job is to be aware of these things and to get to know the names of the children in the class. You also need to know about your class teacher's routines and commitments in the school.

When you work with your class teacher he or she will be responsible for:

- **showing you class rules and procedures (often by example);**
- **modelling good practice in teaching;**
- **helping you to analyse and reflect on your practice;**
- **focusing your attention on pupils' learning;**
- **discussing your planning so that it meets the school's needs as well as yours, and helping you to pitch it right.**

Your class teacher may also:

- **observe lessons on an agreed basis, possibly with your mentor or head teacher;**
- **give you written and oral feedback on your lessons;**
- **help you to develop self-evaluation strategies;**
- **monitor your files.**

Your class teacher is your colleague, your model and your adviser. He or she will have a unique teaching style and by observing it you can learn valuable lessons. As you progress in your practice, the teacher will share lesson planning and share the teaching as well as supporting you in planning and teaching lessons.

What to expect of course tutors

The role of the course tutor, from a university or another partnership, varies enormously from course to course and they have different titles – advisers, link tutors, visiting tutors, etc. You will need to be sure you know the structure of your course. Roles of the course tutors in school based training may include:

- **ensuring your setting meets your training needs;**
- **target-setting and approval;**
- **reviewing progress and targets;**
- **visiting the placement to observe your teaching and giving feedback;**
- **offering support for subject knowledge improvement;**
- **offering advice about teaching techniques;**
- **moderating mentor assessment and grading of your performance;**
- **offering support for the mentor in your training and assessment.**

Target-setting or approval

In all courses you will be expected to set targets for your teaching and agree these with either a course tutor or your school mentor. This is part of your personal professional development. These targets are discussed in more detail later, but you will be expected to link them to the Teachers' Standards. As you progress through your placement you will modify and add to your targets as you achieve some of them. See target-setting (Chapter 7).

Reviewing progress and targets

When you have completed a period of school based training or placement you need to review your progress against the targets you set and the Teachers' Standards. Use your training report, any written feedback you have had, your file of plans and evaluations. Your course tutor (or mentor) may meet you to help you review the placement: if so, make sure you go to the meeting prepared. Make a frank assessment of whether or not you have met your targets and how well you have done. Identify the standards you still have to address. Consider your strengths and your weaknesses. As well as identifying targets, your tutors can help you identify what you should do to meet them. By engaging in this type of review you are addressing the standards outlined in the Preamble to the Teachers' Standards and also Standard 8, by acting professionally to improve your performance.

Visiting the school, observing your teaching and giving feedback

Course tutors from a university or from other schools in the partnership will usually arrange to visit you on placement at least once. There will probably be a number of reasons for the visit. They will want to monitor:

- **that you are well placed and that the placement is meeting your needs;**
- **that you are making progress on your placement by building up your planning, teaching and assessment experience;**
- **that you are reviewing and achieving your targets;**
- **that you and your mentor are making the arrangements necessary to meet your targets;**
- **that you are doing any tasks you have been asked to do;**
- **that you are developing confidence;**
- **that your mentor is happy with your progress.**

Support for subject knowledge improvement and teaching techniques

A visiting tutor may be able to suggest experiences you need to develop your teaching or subject knowledge. For instance, you might need to begin to teach the mental/oral section of a maths lesson, to observe National Tests in another year group or to discuss the Early Years Foundation Profile with the Reception teacher. These arrangements can be made with your mentor.

Moderating mentor assessment and grading of your performance

On most courses, a tutor will visit to observe a lesson you are teaching. The tutor may do a joint observation with the mentor or teacher. This serves two purposes. First, the mentor and course tutor will offer you written feedback to assist your target-setting. Second, a joint observation will also have moderation value in the placement, ensuring that the tutor and mentor share opinions about your practice and expectations about what you should be achieving.

Support for the mentor

Course tutors will see many teachers and trainees teaching. They can help mentors to pinpoint the most effective experiences for you.

In some courses you may find these course roles split so that a personal tutor helps you set targets whilst an advisor visits you in school. Be sure you check the role of the course tutors in your placement for your particular course.

What the school is expecting of you

The school is committed to ITT so they are looking forward to your placement. The Preamble of the Teachers' Standards (2013) tells you what is expected of you as a teacher:

> *Teachers make the education of their pupils their first concern, and are accountable for achieving the highest possible standards in work and conduct. Teachers act with honesty and integrity; have strong subject knowledge; keep their knowledge and skills as teachers up-to-date and are self-critical; forge positive professional relationships; and work with parents in the best interests of their pupils.*

This is a demanding list, and you need to show that you are striving to achieve it. Your mentor will be looking for a professional attitude: most mentors would cite this as your most important quality. What is a professional attitude? It is the hallmark of a professional (of any type) that they aim to review and improve their work, develop their skills and abilities and take responsibility for their work and professional development. In addition:

- **You need to be enthusiastic and committed to your chosen training. Enthusiasm and commitment produce positive responses from staff and pupils alike.**
- **You need to show your enthusiasm and commitment by being well prepared and working hard. This will earn the respect and support of your colleagues and make your lessons go well. Nothing upsets colleagues more than a trainee who is constantly trying to avoid work or leave early.**
- **You need to be willing to ask for help and information in a polite and friendly manner, and to choose an appropriate person and moment to do so.**
- **You need to be sensitive to the stresses that all teachers occasionally feel – five minutes before a tricky lesson is not the time to ask the teacher of that lesson for help.**
- **You need to be reasonably self-critical and able to accept criticism and advice as a learning experience. No one learns without some less-than-perfect lessons. No one will expect you to have all the answers.**
- **You need to feel you are directing your training and balancing your needs with the needs of the teachers and children. No one will respect you if, at the end of a placement, you have not done specific tasks because you 'didn't get round to it'.**

Evidence of a professional attitude comes from a number of signs that you give in the early contacts with the school. Some of these are mentioned in Part Two of the Teachers' Standards: 'Teachers must have proper and professional regard for the ethos, policies and practices of the school in which they teach, and maintain high standards in their own attendance and punctuality' (Teachers' Standards, Part Two, p.14). Appropriate dress is important. Different schools have different codes of dress for staff and these are usually unspoken rules. On your first visit it is worth being smart, but practical. Look at how the other teachers dress (perhaps on the school website). You will be setting an example to the children on behalf of the school and representing the school's values. Do not dress in a way that might upset children, parents or colleagues. Avoid immodest clothes and unusual hairstyles and remove obvious piercings. You will need to consider certain aspects of appearance for health and safety reasons. Long hair needs to be held back so that you have a clear all-round view, otherwise you cannot do the job. Your nails need to be short enough to help children in, say, gymnastics, without spiking them. Dress like a member of the profession you want to join, but do not feel you have to be super smart or purchase a whole new wardrobe.

Punctuality is also extremely important. Although the children will probably arrive between 8.30 and 8.55 a.m., the staff will be arriving at school much earlier. If you arrange to arrive early at school in order to meet your mentor, he or she will have set aside some time for you. That time is precious so make sure you are there and ready to make the most of it.

When you begin your teacher training, you sign up to Part Two of the Teachers' Standards, which define the behaviour and attitudes that set the required standard of conduct throughout your career.

Teachers uphold public trust in the profession and maintain high standards of ethics and behaviour, within and outside school, by:

- o *treating pupils with dignity, building relationships rooted in mutual respect, and at all times observing proper boundaries appropriate to a teacher's professional position*

- o *having regard for the need to safeguard pupils' well-being, in accordance with statutory provisions*

- o *showing tolerance of and respect for the rights of others*

- o *not undermining fundamental British values, including democracy, the rule of law, individual liberty and mutual respect, and tolerance of those with different faiths and beliefs*

- o *ensuring that personal beliefs are not expressed in ways which exploit pupils' vulnerability or might lead them to break the law.*

(Teachers' Standards, 2013, Part Two, p. 14)

These requirements affect you from your very first day in school and circumscribe the ways you interact with pupils and the views you express. Though almost all trainee teachers understand this in their face-to-face relationships, social media is also important and you are responsible for your internet conduct. This means you must check your internet and social media presence regularly (and you may have done this before you applied for teacher training). You must make sure that you present yourself, through words and pictures, in ways that are acceptable to colleagues, parents and pupils. Respecting proper boundaries appropriate to a teacher's professional position means you follow the school social media and communications policy. Usually, this means that your pupils and parents should not be 'friends' on personal social media sites. You should not give pupils your home mobile number and you should use your school or university email address for professional correspondence.

MINI CASE MINI CASE MINI CASE **MINI CASE** MINI CASE **MINI CASE**

As part of inducting Paula into a KS2 placement, her school searched her name on the internet. Her social media pages were accessible and senior teachers saw her posts. Unfortunately, Paula had expressed her views about her Polish ex-boyfriend in ways the Head saw as racist and offensive and Paula was asked to leave the school.

Confidentiality is another important professional characteristic. As a trainee teacher you must show the same degree of confidentiality that is expected of other teachers. This means that what happens in school is confidential within the school. You can usually talk and write about school events within the training partnership. You would certainly want to do so in course essays, for example, but even then names of children, staff and schools should be disguised. You need to express yourself professionally and not make unsupported, sweeping or uninformed judgements.

In discussions within school you should avoid criticising your fellow teachers and gossiping about colleagues. This is just as important outside the staff group. Staff rooms contain a good many adults who are not members of school staff – visiting parents, advisers, inspectors, etc., and you need to remember this. You should not discuss school inappropriately with friends or relations. The perils of gossip extend to social media. You must be very circumspect about what you share and who can see it. It is unprofessional to discuss school matters, teachers or pupils online and you can do untold damage to colleagues, teachers and pupils with an unguarded post or tweet.

MINI CASE MINI CASE **MINI CASE** **MINI CASE** MINI CASE **MINI CASE** **MINI CASE**

The importance of confidentiality was brought home to Christine, a third-year BA student, in an uncomfortable way. Christine had undertaken a placement in the school the previous term and had discussed it with a friend whose child attended the placement school. At some point Christine unwittingly expressed a negative opinion of the teaching skills of Mr X. The following term Christine's friend approached the school and asked that her son should not be put into Mr X's class because of what she had heard. Naturally, the head teacher of the school was very upset. She felt that Christine had acted unprofessionally and damaged the reputation of the school. Christine was aghast and realised that she had, unintentionally, acted extremely unprofessionally. This was certainly not the sort of evidence of team working and collaboration she wanted to accumulate towards meeting The Standards. She could only write apologising to the school and learn a hard lesson.

All this seems a tall order at first, but as long as you go to school positive and well prepared, you will find your school welcoming. Your school has the right to expect you to start your school based training with:

- a developing knowledge of the Teachers' Standards against which you will be assessed;
- an informed knowledge about your course of training – you should have read your course and placement details on the website or in a handbook;
- a clear idea of what your targets are for this period of school based training. (On first placements or right at the start of a school based course of training this is much harder than in subsequent placements because everything is a target. Do not be afraid to discuss it with your mentor and set narrower targets such as specific observations or taking parts of lessons.)
- a clear picture of what you want to get out of this block of school based training, not just from the point of view of the course and the standards, but on a personal level;
- an expectation of participating in assessment and planning meetings;
- an expectation of participating in staff meetings and training days, although you may not have much to contribute at first;
- your training plan or record of professional development;
- a teaching file.

REFLECTIVE TASK

Prepare your documentation for school based training. You will usually have a teaching file (sometimes called a placement or teaching practice file) and a file about your professional development such as a professional development plan or record of professional development. You might be asked to combine these.

Prepare your teaching file

This is a file that you will use day to day to hold notes on school policies, plans, evaluations, assessments, etc. At first your teaching file will not contain a great deal but it will indicate that you have given some thought to your school based training and begun your preparation. When setting up a teaching file you need to read the course documentation very carefully and think about your targets. This will help you to decide the sections you will need in a file and how to arrange them. Before you get to school a teaching file may simply have the following:

- your details;
- details of the school (including OFSTED reports);
- file dividers for various sections (school policies, medium-term plans, weekly plans, daily plans, lesson evaluations, assessments, notes of mentor meetings, etc.);
- course details, including relevant sections of the course information;
- any forms needed for this block of school based training, possibly as part of your record of professional development or training plan.

This is not in-depth material, but it is a strong indicator of your attitude. A trainee who arranges this before the school based training starts sends out strong messages of positive professional values, such as organisation. It shows you are committed and willing to work hard.

Prepare your training plan file (or professional development profile)

This document will have your background details in it, the Teachers' Standards and will develop to form a full record of your training. This file will probably be where you record the targets you set for this block of school based training with the mentor or link tutor. At the start of a period of school based training or placement you should expect to spend some time reviewing this record. Use the format you are given as part of your training to:

- identify what you have already achieved in relation to the standards;
- identify key standards which you aim to meet.

You will discuss your record with your mentor at the school of the block of school based training or at an agreed point (usually termly).

You will do a good deal more with this file when you have finished this block of school based training, when you may want to put lesson plans, lesson observations, assessments and photographs into it.

Union membership

Most teachers belong to one of the main teaching unions (contact details on page 38). These are trade unions that negotiate on behalf of their members on issues such as pay and conditions. However, the unions also offer a wider range of additional services. Most of the unions produce materials especially for trainee teachers and NQTs. These range from advice about classroom management, to tips for getting a job. The publications are often free to trainees and many trainees have found them invaluable. The unions also offer services such as insurance cover as part of membership. Each package is different but may provide insurance cover for:

- **personal accidents;**
- **hospitalisation;**
- **personal property (including spectacles);**
- **malicious damage to motor vehicles on school or college premises.**

The membership may also include the union's legal services in the case of any dispute and the services of the union in agreeing your pay package when you take up a job.

There are also additional benefits such as:

- **discount shopping;**
- **life assurance and investments;**
- **mortgage facilities;**
- **legal services;**
- **credit card facilities;**
- **personal loans;**
- **motor insurance;**
- **motor breakdown and recovery services;**
- **travel facilities;**
- **tax recovery services;**
- **magazines;**
- **pocket diaries, calendars and pens, etc.**

We strongly recommend you join at least one union before going into school for the insurance benefits, as well as the excellent advice. Membership is usually free for trainees and some NQTs. Each union has slightly different policies and, eventually, you will want to be a member of a union that represents your view but, as a trainee, you do not have to make a final decision about which union to join because you can join them all. The university or partnership running your course may well have arranged contact with the unions. If not, they can be contacted at the URLs listed below.

The unions will have local branches and you may find that in many schools all the staff belong to one union but you can decide about this when you are an NQT.

MINI CASE MINI CASE MINI CASE **MINI CASE** MINI CASE MINI CASE **MINI CASE**

I only joined the unions because they were all there in the university one day and they were giving out good leaflets and pens and I really didn't expect to need them. On my very first term training in school my car was badly scratched in the school car park. On school based training you are quite tense anyway and I found it really upsetting. I had already had a recent insurance claim and risked losing my no claims bonus if I claimed on the car policy. I also didn't want to make a fuss in school or draw attention to myself. The union said I was covered through them and they paid out for the repairs with very little effort on my part. Since then I have had the magazines and booklets they send, which have been good, especially in helping me to prepare interviews. I also consulted them about my starting salary. I will retain membership of all three unions this (my NQT) year then decide which to go for when I have to pay.

Nahid, NQT

A SUMMARY OF KEY POINTS

- Your school based training schools are chosen with your training needs and circumstances in mind and should include a range of experiences for you.

- You should do a little research about your school before you start.

- You should write to your school and introduce yourself as a professional, enthusiastic trainee.

- Your mentor is a member of the school staff who will know about your training and will work to support you through your school based training or placement.

- Your class teacher will be your principal model of good practice and will teach with you.

- Course tutors (if you have them) will participate in your training, moderating, offering advice and training.

- From the very beginning of your school based training you must act professionally. This means having a professional attitude, being punctual, maintaining confidentiality and dressing appropriately.

- We strongly suggest you join at least one teaching union before beginning school based training.

RESOURCES RESOURCES **RESOURCES** RESOURCES RESOURCES **RESOURCES**

Association of Teachers and Lecturers. ATL, formerly the Assistant Masters and Mistresses Association (AMMA), is a fully democratic, TUC-affiliated trade union and professional association. www.atl.org.uk

Educational Institute of Scotland. The EIS is the largest organisation of teachers and lecturers in Scotland representing around 80 per cent of the profession in nursery, primary, special, secondary and further and higher education. www.eis.org.uk/

National Association of School Masters/Union of Women Teachers. NASUWT is one of the largest teaching unions and the only one to organise in England, Wales, Scotland and Northern Ireland. NASUWT has members in all sectors of education and represents teachers in all roles including heads and deputies. www.teachersunion.org.uk

National Union of Teachers. The NUT is the largest of all the teaching unions. It is a professional association and a trade union that also provides access to a variety of conferences and reference materials for teachers and staff within the education sector. Membership for students is free. www.teachers.org.uk/index.php

Professional Association of Teachers. This independent trade union caters for all workers in education. Founded in 1970 it has approximately 35,000 members. www.pat.org.uk

3
Starting in school

Learning outcomes

In this chapter we aim to help you gather information in a setting that is new to you. Even if you have considerable experience in schools you may benefit from taking a close look at the culture and organisation.

By the end of this chapter you should:

- **know the purpose of the first few days you spend in school;**
- **know what to find out about your school;**
- **know what information to collect about your class;**
- **be able to observe in the first days in your class.**

Early days in school

At or before the start of the main body of a block of school based training, or at the start of that placement, you will spend a few days in the school to get used to the setting. This may be one day a week for several weeks, it may be a few days in a single week or you may do a couple of weeks in school in the academic year before you start your school based training. Or you may have been in school for some time and will be focusing on the new class or age phase. However your preparation time is organised, this time is crucial in enabling you to be ready to make the most of a school based training block or placement.

In those first few days it is important to get to know the school and you should expect members of staff to help you to do that. The school mentor will arrange the first few days in a new situation so that you can:

- **tour the school, perhaps with children;**
- **have a copy of the school prospectus;**
- **learn tips about the school routines (such as timetables, playground duty, etc.);**
- **learn the rules for photocopying and use of resources;**
- **see and note the school behaviour and health and safety policies;**
- **learn the first aid procedures;**
- **learn the fire drill procedures (for your class);**
- **set up regular mentor meeting times;**
- **learn about your class.**

Many schools will have a trainee teacher induction pack ready for you. This usually includes:

- **the school prospectus;**
- **guidance given to supply teachers about routines, break times, etc., school behaviour and health and safety policies;**

- a staff list;
- a school map.

If your school does not have such a pack you should ask your mentor for access to these documents.

School layout and emergency exits

It is usual practice for the school mentor to show students around a school on an initial visit but in a large school this can leave you feeling overwhelmed by the sheer amount of information given. It is a good idea to obtain a copy of the school map and ask a small group of older children to take you on an additional tour during a lunch break. In this way you can proceed at your own pace and annotate the map with any notes that will be personally useful. It is also crucial that you know the location of fire exits of the area you will be working in and your assembly point outside the building. Identify these on the map and clarify the procedure for using them with your class teacher. You can build on this information by looking at the school health and safety policy.

Who's who?

When you join a school for school based training, even for a short placement, you become a member of the school team, even if you are a temporary, junior member. Make a conscious effort to become acquainted with not only your class teacher but with other staff too. The school staffing list may be extensive, so make short notes next to names to help you remember who's who. Try to learn names, starting with those of your mentor, teacher, teaching assistant(s) and head teacher and notice how staff members address each other – it would be unfortunate to call your head teacher by his first name if the class teacher always calls him Mr — . A little polite conversation will usually allow you to find out what your mentor's and class teacher's areas of responsibility are within the school, what age group or sets they teach and which parts of their work they enjoy most.

It is essential to know the names and roles of any parallel class teachers and support staff. You will be working closely with them – observing their practice, planning, sharing resources – and may teach lessons with them. You will also want to learn the names of a wider circle of teachers over the first week or so of the placement. The SENCO (Special Educational Needs Co-ordinator) will be an important member of staff who can tell you about processes for children with SEN, show you some of the plans for intervention groups and discuss arrangements made to meet the needs of a range of children. There will also be subject co-ordinators for each subject in the Primary curriculum and for the areas of learning at Foundation Key Stage. Knowing and understanding the roles of colleagues with specific responsibilities is part of The Standards (Part Two, Standard 8) You may want to learn from these members of staff later in the placement by, for instance, observing particularly good guided reading by the literacy co-ordinator or a dance lesson led by the PE co-ordinator. Arrangements of this type are usually made through your mentor and you should discuss them with your mentor in the first instance.

Look beyond the classroom and introduce yourself to staff in the office and the lunch-time supervisors who work directly with the children. This will allow you to appreciate the school community properly, and established, knowledgeable staff are more likely to support and advise a student who makes an effort to be friendly than one who shuts themselves away in their classroom.

Important routines – assemblies, playground duties and lunchtime

One of the most important, and obvious, pieces of information you need is the timing of the school day. This information may well be in your welcome pack but if it is not, make sure you note on your first day:

- **school starting and finishing times;**
- **when staff arrive and leave the school;**
- **the times of break times and lunchtime;**
- **assembly times;**
- **the weekly staff meeting time;**
- **any regular phase or planning meetings.**

These form the basic structure of the day but you will also want to observe the teachers' routines over your first week. Most teachers arrive some time before the children start and leave some time after school finishes. They will all stay on to attend the weekly staff meeting. You should expect to do the same and you may well find that, early in your career, you need extra time to accomplish your preparation. If your school has staff training days for the whole school staff it is important that you take part in these, although as a trainee you should expect to keep a low profile. Participating in these aspects of school life shows your professional commitment.

Try to observe and learn the school's social rituals. On your first day ask what the arrangements are for paying for coffee and tea, and offer to contribute. Notice when the teachers congregate in the staff room and when they stay in their rooms to pre-pare. There will not be time for you to leave school premises during the day. Do not expect to be able to pop out to the shops at lunchtime or make personal arrangements during school time. If school staff bring a packed lunch or have school dinners, do the same. Most teachers spend a very short time in the staff room at lunchtime but they will usually choose the same times to do their preparation and all use the beginning, middle or end part of lunchtime to congregate in the staff room. It is important to participate gradually in these routines. In a Nursery there may be very little time at break time or lunchtime and staff may have a rota for these occasions. It is important to notice when the staff do meet to chat and mentors will see your willingness to participate as part of Part Two, Standard 8 – developing effective professional relationships with colleagues.

There will be wider opportunities for child-orientated activities. Breakfast and after-school clubs are common and you should find out about them. You will also, gradually, want to find out about any after school or lunchtime activities. Your knowledge of French, chess, rugby or ballroom dancing might be useful and allow you to contribute later in the placement.

We'd all made the usual jokes about not sitting in the deputy head's chair before the course got going but, really, going into the staff room for the first couple of times in both my schools was a bit nerve wracking. My first school was huge and the staff room seemed vast. I felt very conspicuous. Everyone pretty much ignored me and just made their own tea and put the cups in the dishwasher. My mentor sort of waved me on and said 'help yourself'. I didn't say a word for the first few times in there, but gradually I found I could join in the general chit chat. The staff sort of included me and I can see, looking back, that their lack of fuss was actually reassuring. I didn't spend much time in the staff room – about 15 to 20 minutes at lunchtime, maximum – but after five weeks I was really at home. I see now how important it was to be part of the staff in that way.

Jennie, PGCE

I had been a TA, so I was used to schools but I did find I talked about different things in the staff room during my placements. In a few minutes at lunchtime I could ask all sorts of things and sort out resources. I enjoyed the familiarity but it felt different.

John, SCITT trainee

My placement was in a Nursery school so even with the nursery nurses and teachers on a rota there were only really three of us in the staff room at lunchtime or on breaks. I was surprised that this worked so well, but it did mean that planning meetings were even more important. I think that it is really vital to remember to take your breaks for tea and keep your energy levels up.

Pat, BA student

All teachers are involved in some routine duties such as playground or corridor supervision or bus loading duties. These are important times for supervision of the children but most of all a very important time for you to see the children outside the very formal setting of the class. You should go with your class teacher when they do these duties. If they do not do playground duty, arrange through your mentor to go out with another teacher.

Do a playground duty with another teacher (Key Stage 1 or 2). Choose a day when you have already met your class and know them a little.

As you go out ask:

- **How often does the teacher do playground duty?**
- **What is his/her main purpose in doing duty?**
- **What are the behaviour rules for children in the playground?**
- **What, if any, equipment is provided?**
- **Who is the first-aider and what is the procedure for cuts and grazes?**

Notice how the teacher circulates round the area and talks to groups of children.

- **How does the teacher appear friendly with them?**
- **How does the teacher, at the same time, maintain a professional relationship?**

You need to actively imitate these strategies so that the children will chat with you but not be too familiar. You should discourage gratuitous cuddling, children's hands in your pockets and over-personal questions. Children will try these as ways to test your role as a teacher.

Observe the children at play. For many of them, playtime is the most important part of the day and it is certainly the time when most social learning is going on – how to make and keep friends, turn taking, joining and leaving groups, negotiation and compromise. Playtime may also involve a little mild violence or psychological torture (mostly about friendship) and you have a role here in preventing bullying and helping children to sort things out.

Observe what the children do at playtime.

- **Do different groups do different things?**
- **Does there seem to be a difference in activity related to age or gender?**
- **Look at children you know and see who plays together.**
- **Are there any children on their own? Do they seem happy?**
- **Who complains of being left out? How can you help them to take part?**
- **Are the children using the equipment – climbing toys, sand pits, markings, skipping ropes, etc.?**
- **Which children use them?**
- **What games are being played (ball rhymes, skipping rhymes, variations on tag, etc.)?**

Observing your class in the playground can give you a much greater understanding of some children.

Moving around the school and class

Notice how the children move around the school. This is a very rule-governed business and recognising the rules (and when someone is breaking them) is one of the things that identifies you as a teacher to the children. On your first day, notice how the children use the corridors (no running, letting others pass nicely) and be prepared to ask children to do this. There are also basic rules for moving around in your class.

- **In an Early Childhood setting, what are the processes for settling children on the mat?**
- **In a Nursery setting, what are the rules for behaviour on the mat?**
- **During seatwork, when are the children allowed to leave their seats?**
- **When they are sent to get an item in class, how are they supposed to move, and what are the sanctions for running, etc.?**
- **When you want to accomplish a transition such as moving from the mat to groups, what is the procedure and best way to give instructions?**
- **What key words should you include in instructions to move around?**
- **When the teacher sends children to get something, note how he or she avoids all the children rushing to the same place.**
- **What procedure is used when moving into another class or area? Do the children line up?**

- When moving into the hall for PE, do the children do something specific, like finding a space?
- When the teacher sends a child to another place with a message, register or other task, what is the routine? Is it a privileged job? Does more than one child always go?

These are small but important details and observing them will establish your role as a teacher.

MINI CASE MINI CASE **MINI CASE** MINI CASE **MINI CASE** MINI CASE **MINI CASE**

In my first placement I didn't really establish myself with the class and I felt they saw me as a helper – not a teacher at all. It shrivelled my confidence. On my next placement I asked my next mentor for advice before I even went into class. She told me to start by moving groups around as part of the lessons my teacher was teaching that day. I worked with my teacher to do this on my second day. It set me up. I began by showing a bit of authority, with my teacher there to support me, and I built on it. On my third day I lined the class up and took them into the hall for assembly. It took a bit of time to get silence and some naming of individuals to keep it but I felt it was the one act that established my role and set me up for really teaching that class.

Abby, Second Year BA

Taking photographs in school

A small but important aspect of your ICT work will be taking photographs in school. As part of your assessment evidence, especially at the Foundation Key Stage, you (and the children) may well take photographs of children and you will certainly take photographs of assemblies and school visits. These photographs can be shared with the children for discussion, discussed with parents and may go into displays, children's work and school newsletters and websites. The use of photographs is governed by the school policy and professional responsibility. The school will have a policy about the use of photographs that aims to protect the identity of children and of the school. You must read it and adhere to it.

You should also ask your teacher to take photographs of you teaching in a way that adheres to the school photography policy. Photographs of you teaching a class masterfully, using the interactive whiteboard, working sensitively in the dramatic play area, reading with a group, accompanying a school visit or assisting at cookery are not only excellent in supporting your evidence towards the Teachers' Standards, but also go down very well at interviews for teaching posts.

When you use photographs of yourself teaching for displays, ensure that no children are identifiable and that the school name cannot be identified from the photographs. If it is on the school sweatshirt you may have an interesting IT challenge smudging this part of the image.

Your class group(s)

In any block of school based training you will have a key teacher and class but this might mean different things in different settings.

Early Years settings have a number of different ways of organising their work. All of them will involve teachers and nursery practitioners planning together and teaching together.

- **Nursery classes can be an ordinary class in the school with a nursery teacher and nursery nurse.**
- **Nursery classes may be part time or have two shifts of children, those who come in the morning and those who come in the afternoon, with a few who stay all day.**
- **Early Childhood settings may be organised as Foundation Key Stage units. This might mean a combined Nursery and Reception unit in which all the children from both years work together. These units may have two teachers and a number of nursery practitioners or one teacher and more nursery practitioners.**

Whatever the organisation, you will be assigned to one teacher and will be gradually taking over his or her role in the planning, teaching, management and assessment of this class. For Early Years this means working very closely with the team of nursery practitioners or teaching assistants and you will have to be very careful to identify the teacher's special role in the team. This is not as easy as it sounds.

In Key Stage 1 classes you may find a number of ways of organising. Classes will not usually exceed 30 children, and most of them will have a single teacher and a part-time or full-time teaching assistant.

- **A simple Year 1 or Year 2 class with one teacher is probably the most common organisation.**
- **Many classes will be mixed years, with Reception children (who are doing the Early Years Foundation Stage curriculum) and Year 1, or Year 1 and Year 2 together. Mixed year groups make planning a little more challenging.**
- **Some schools choose vertical or family grouping as a matter of principle. In these schools there may be a number of Key Stage 1 classes all organised to include Year 1, Year 2 and sometimes Year 3 children.**
- **In a very few Key Stage 1 settings, usually in larger schools with multiple form entry, there will be sets where children are re-grouped across the classes for a particular subject (often mathematics or English). You will usually work with the sets your teacher takes and have the extra challenge of getting to know a larger number of children.**
- **Some larger Key Stage 1 settings may organise the children into home groups with a teacher responsible for up to 30 children but the curriculum will be organised over a number of rooms or areas such as the literacy area, maths area, creative area, etc. Each teacher may plan for and teach one area. In this case you will stick with your teacher for home group time and work in different areas at different times to get experience across the curriculum.**

In Key Stage 2 you may have classes of over 30 pupils. Each class has a teacher and some time from a classroom assistant. You may have:

- **a single year class that does all subjects with the teacher;**
- **a single year class that does most subjects with the teacher but has some specialist teaching in music, PE or some other subject;**
- **a mixed year class that may do all subjects, or some with the same teacher;**
- **mixed year or single year classes that set for English, mathematics and sometimes science.**

This is very common in Key Stage 2, especially in schools with more than one form entry. In practice it means that the children all go to pre-arranged classes for mathematics and English at an agreed time. The sets may be organised by ability and children may be in different sets for English and mathematics. You will usually work with the set for which your class teacher has responsibility but your training needs might require that you work with a different set. For example, if you wanted to develop your differentiation for able pupils, you might work with a top set.

Meeting the class

Whatever class you are placed in, your first step will be meeting the class teacher and simply watching the class for a day, perhaps helping children to complete tasks. Your introduction to the class is very important. The children will use your title and surname (unless first names are used for all teachers in the school) and the teacher will tell the children you will be teaching them for some of this term. You must look confident and relaxed, however terrified you feel, and fill the role of teacher as you are introduced. Stand up straight and keep your arms relaxed (it may help to hold a file or something to stop you nervously clasping your hands). Smile – a relaxed, authoritative smile is appropriate, not a nervous whimper or a rictus grin. Any time you say something it must be confident and authoritative: 'I am looking forward to teaching you' rather than a weak 'Hello'. First impressions count and you need to signal to the class that you know what you are doing – even if you are not really that sure of yourself.

During your first few days or on visits, obtain class lists for all the groups of children you will be working with. Then take time to annotate these lists from your observations and in discussion with the class teacher. His or her observations will be very useful and enable you to begin to formulate a class picture before actually working with the children. The checklist below suggests possible queries for you to observe or discuss with your class teacher.

- How many children are there in the class?
- Who is full time/part time/morning or afternoon (for Nursery)?
- What sets are there and who is in which set?
- How are the class seated? Do they choose a spot or are they assigned chairs? If they generally stay in the same places, making a seating map will help you learn names.
- Which children are on the school's SEN register? How does their special need manifest itself? How does the class teacher plan for inclusion?
- Which children in the class have been identified as gifted and talented on the school's register? In which subject(s) is the child gifted or talented? What strategies does the class teacher utilise to ensure they are reaching their full potential?
- Which children have EAL? What other language do they speak? What arrangements are made to support them?
- Which children find difficulty in controlling their behaviour? Is this related to an identified SEN? What steps does the class teacher take to manage the child's behaviour? Is there a reward system? What will happen if the child needs to be removed from the classroom as a result of its behaviour?
- Are there any sensitive issues about any child's family circumstances you need to be aware of (e.g. recent bereavement, divorce, parental custody or child protection concerns)? Remember you are expected to treat this information with the highest degree of confidentiality.
- Are there any children with medical problems that you should be aware of? For example are there any children with asthma, epilepsy or allergies? Where are the inhalers kept? Who is qualified to administer a child's epi-pen? Who are the school's first-aiders? What procedure should you follow if a medical incident occurs during your lesson?
- Which friendship groupings are conducive to learning and which are not?

- **What teaching assistance does the teacher have? When do teaching assistants work with the class? When do teaching assistants work with particular children? What are the roles of teaching assistants in this class? Are there any other adults working in the class?**

As you spend your first day in the class you will begin to learn children's names and to see how they work.

PRACTICAL TASK PRACTICAL TASK PRACTICAL TASK PRACTICAL TASK PRACTICAL TASK

Observe a daily routine. On the first day in school you need to note as many class routines as you can. Use one of these question lists to guide your first observations, then supplement these in discussion with your teacher. Make a note of times at each transition point.

Early Years setting

- How (and when) do the children come into the building?
- How do staff greet parents and how long do parents stay?
- Is the first activity of the day set up? When? By whom?
- How do children know where to go?
- Which adults manage which tasks? Who is outside?
- Are outdoor clothes such as wellington boots and coats used? What is the routine?
- How do adults participate in play tasks?
- How is a change of task signalled? (Music, clapping, hands in air, etc.)
- How many children are allowed to do each activity at a time? How do they know?
- What is the routine for fruit time? Who prepares it? What do the children do? What language is used?
- What are the routines for using the lavatory and hand washing? (If any children in the setting wear nappies, ask your teacher for advice.)
- When do the children gather for group (or class) time on the mat?
- What do children do for packing up time? How is this signalled?
- When are stories and rhyme routines done?
- What arrangements are there for children taking books home (or story sacks) and changing them?

Key Stage 1 or 2

- How (and when) do children come in from the playground and what are they expected to do as they come in?
- How does the teacher settle the class to attention?
- Who takes the register? How do children respond? What do the children do as it is taken? What happens to the register?
- Is there an assembly? Does the teacher attend?
- What are the lesson times?
- How does each lesson start and finish?
- Which other adults work in the class during teaching times and what do they do?
- How are resources (pencils, books, etc.) arranged? Who collects them?
- How does the teacher get the children's attention?
- How does the teacher move children from the mat to tables?

Timetable, curriculum, resources and behaviour

In your first few days you will have the chance to talk to your mentor and your teacher.

Your mentor will play a lead role in the school's involvement in the partnership for training. This means the mentor will be familiar with the Teachers' Standards, even if the rest of the staff are not. Your mentor will also have contact with the university or school alliance involved in your training. So your mentor will know the arrangements for your training and the requirements (generally) of this block of school based training – which key stage you need to be in, when you will be arriving and something of your previous experience. The mentor will also know their role in helping you to become established, observing, arranging meetings with you and reviewing progress. Usually, the mentor will have the report forms that may be required about your progress, but in some courses you will take these into school yourself.

The mentor may have some reports on previous blocks of school based training and you may have sent a letter about yourself. Your mentor will be keen to know a little more about you and will certainly want to set, or see, specific targets for this placement. On some courses, you may decide on these with a course tutor before the school based training. In others you will set these with the mentor early in the placement. Either way, meeting these targets, showing your mentor evidence that you have met the targets, and setting new targets are important elements of your relationship. So your first mentor meeting will focus on:

- **discussing the requirements for this block of school based training or placement and personal targets for your placement;**
- **helping you to get information about the school;**
- **answering your questions so far.**

You will also meet your teacher. Key topics for discussion with him/her will be the timetable of the class, planning for class teaching and managing behaviour.

Having observed for a day in Key Stage 1 or 2, you will have ideas about the rough timings of the day. To draw up a timetable you need to check these and add hall and PE times, times when any sets meet, times when the class is booked into a computer suite or has use of a set of laptops (or tablets) and times when other teachers take the class. You can then put in the teacher's intended teaching times. These may be simply English, mathematics and cross-curricular themes, or each subject may have an identified time. Many schools block some subjects into different terms, so your class may do history one term and geography the next. You will also need to know what teaching assistance you have in and out of the classroom and who will work with children during your lessons.

In Early Years Foundation Stage you will have a broad idea of the pattern of activity from observation and you need to discuss with the teacher how the core and specific areas of learning are addressed. Do different staff manage different areas? Does each member of staff plan activities for each area? You need to know which activities the children are encouraged to do and which are a matter of choice. How is this monitored?

The planning of the teaching is your next area of interest. Establish what topics are to be taught and what associated learning objectives need to be achieved in each curriculum subject during your placement. Obtain copies of any relevant medium- and short-term plans and look at these with your class teacher. He or she will identify lessons for you to observe and be sure you know whether you are expected to take part in them. Planning is discussed in more detail in Chapter 4.

When you have identified the lessons, or parts of lessons, you will teach on the timetable it is essential to be prepared. The following checklist will help.

- **Find out where the school stores the curriculum resources (this will take a little time). Which resources are classroom based and which are kept centrally? Once located, you can select resources applicable to your identified teaching objectives and refer to them in your planning.**
- **What computers are available? Will you have an electronic whiteboard, computers or tablets in the class, laptops or access to a set of laptops? In the first few days at school arrange a time with the IT co-ordinator to examine how the school manages its toolbox of software.**
- **Assess whether new resources need to be made in order to achieve the learning objective. Any new resources you create should be relevant and child friendly.**
- **Is a worksheet necessary? If so, when you create it make sure it allows children to demonstrate their understanding rather than just filling in boxes.**
- **If you need to use photocopied resources for your lesson find out the school's procedure for photo-copying. Will administration staff or teaching assistants organise photocopying for teaching staff or is it the teacher's responsibility? If it is the latter, make time to understand how the photocopier works.**
- **Who will help to prepare and locate resources and create displays? If you have a certain amount of administrative or teaching assistant time you need to know how much time you have and to whom you should go. You also need to identify areas for your displays with the teacher.**
- **Be organised. Ensure your resources are ready before the lesson. Photocopy any material in plenty of time. Photocopiers have a habit of jamming, usually just before an observed lesson, so have your copied resources ready well in advance. Collect any centrally stored resources, such as lenses for a science lesson, well in advance. This will avoid a potentially stressful situation when you realise ten minutes before a lesson that they have disappeared from the science cupboard.**

Teaching a class of children in your first block of school based training can be a daunting process, so if you take steps to be planned and prepared you can focus on developing your classroom management style without the additional worry of lesson content.

REFLECTIVE TASK
REFLECTIVE TASK

When you have done your initial days in your school based training setting you should ask your-self how well you can address the Teachers' Standard which demands that: 'Teachers must have proper and professional regard for the ethos, policies and practices of the school in which they teach' (Teachers' Standards Part 2, p.14).

Organise your notes under these headings:

- **school policies;**
- **the school day (routines);**
- **rules of behaviour;**
- **learning needs of the classes;**
- **resources.**

Review these notes at the end of your first week in school and ensure you have no gaps.

A SUMMARY OF KEY POINTS

- It is essential for you to spend a few days in school to gather information about the school and class.
- You may be placed with one year group but a number of other arrangements are possible, including sets, units and mixed age years.
- Find out about the school policies and read them early in your placement – all activity in school has to follow these policies.
- When you meet your class, create a professional, confident first impression.
- Learn school routines and staff habits. This will help you to feel at home.
- You should learn staff names and roles as soon as possible as you will be working with a number of people in school.
- In your first few days in school you should work out the class timetable and how you will fit in.

RESODRCES RESOURCES RESOURCES RESOURCES RESOURCES RESOURCES

You should make sure you know the curriculum documentation relevant to your class and subjects. These can be found at the Department for Education website at: https://www.gov.uk/government/collections/national-curriculum. This site contains information about the curriculum and assessment and also all the relevant documents.

The equivalent documents for Wales can be found at: http://wales.gov.uk/topics/educationandskills/schoolshome/curriculuminwales/ ?lang=en

Documents for Northern Ireland are at http://www.nicurriculum.org.uk/

Documents for Scotland are at: http://www.scotland.gov.uk/Topics/Education/Schools/curriculum

4

Learning to observe, plan and evaluate in school based training

Learning outcomes

By the end of this chapter you should know:

- how to observe in a focused way;
- how medium-term, short-term and lesson plans are related;
- how to plan for parts of lessons and whole lessons;
- how to evaluate your lessons.

When you have been in your school for a few days, whether it is your first or second school, you will have collected a great deal of information and be ready to focus on the process of learning to teach successfully and meet the Teachers' Standards. Just as each school is different, each trainee is different. You will have a different background, different needs and so will require different experiences from your colleagues. The main techniques you will use to develop your teaching will be:

- observation and discussion with teachers;
- planning;
- evaluating;
- teaching;
- assessing;
- completing school based tasks.

This chapter addresses observation, planning and evaluation.

Observation

Observation in your school based training class(es) is particularly important because it is observation of what you are going to be doing very soon. The key thing to remember in all observations is that you are not observing to judge or criticise in a negative sense. You are observing to see:

- what children and teachers do in certain situations and with certain children;
- how certain actions and situations produce certain responses;
- how policies and theories work in practice;
- what you can learn from the situation.

- The last point is the most important. You will not teach in the same way as anyone you watch but you will learn something from every lesson you observe. At the start of your work in a particular class there is something to be said for aping the teacher – or at least stepping into their shoes. The children in your class are used to certain routines and behaviours from their teacher, so you will appear authoritative and trustworthy to the children if you know the routines and behave as they expect a teacher to behave.
- The observation aspect of school based training is extremely important so do not rush through it. At the start of your time in a class you really need to observe everything – behaviour management, core subject teaching, assemblies, cross-curricular teaching, and staff meetings. Generally, you should observe a subject being taught before you teach it yourself. Some trainees overlook this in their enthusiasm to get going on the teaching part of the training.

General observations

Early in a block of school based training, you should do the following observations, making specific notes, then review your notes. These will enable you to make a start at teaching.

PRACTICAL TASK PRACTICAL TASK PRACTICAL TASK PRACTICAL TASK PRACTICAL TASK

Observing core subject lessons

Key Stage 1 and 2 – observe an English lesson and a maths lesson

Use the form below as a prompt to observe the lesson. Make notes (or use a sheet of a similar layout) about as much as you can so that you get an idea of the structure the teacher and children are used to, the key vocabulary, how arrangements are made for different children's needs and what the routines of the lessons are.

Table 4.1

Prompt sheet for observing literacy and maths		
Lesson objective	Year	No. of children ....
At the beginning of the lesson		
Teaching strategies	Class management	
How does the teacher introduce the lesson objective?	How does the teacher gain the children's attention and settle them?	
Does the teacher check prior knowledge, recall of previous material?	How does the teacher keep attention?	
How is the lesson set out to facilitate the start?	What does the teacher do if a child is not paying attention?	
Resources used?	Evidence of pupils' interest and motivation?	
What do other adults in class do? Modelling of reading or writing?		
Mathematics games? Questioning?		
What is the balance of teacher-to-pupil talk?		
How long does this phase of the lesson last?		

During the lesson	
How do the pupils know what they will be doing?	How does the teacher manage the transition from the mat (or group) to seatwork?
What sorts of tasks are they doing?	
Does the teacher work with one group or many?	How do pupils get their resources?
How do the other adults in the classroom work and with whom?	How does the teacher keep pupils on task?
Is there use of specific vocabulary?	How does the teacher monitor the class?
How are the pupils grouped?	What 'rewards' does the teacher offer? (praise, eye contact, words, etc.)
How are independent tasks related to the rest of the lesson?	
How long does this phase of the lesson last?	What sanctions does the teacher use? (frown, naming, etc.)
At the end of the lesson	
How does the teacher conclude the lesson?	What is the signal for this phase of the lesson?
What learning does the teacher revisit?	
Which pupils report back on what they have done?	How do pupils arrange their resources?
How do pupils know how well they have done?	How does the teacher manage the transition from seat work to the mat (or group)?
How long does this phase of the lesson last? What do other adults in the class do?	
Is there homework?	Are pupils willing or enthusiastic to present their work?
Is the next lesson referred to?	How does the teacher dismiss the class?

Early Years Foundation Stage – observe the teacher's role in a group session

Use one of the two forms below to observe a small group during one session. The first looks at one child activity, the second a whole session, involving more than one activity – possibly a practitioner-directed activity and a child-led activity. Observe as much as you can so that you get an idea of the routines the teacher and children are used to, the key vocabulary, how arrangements are made to include different children and what the learning objective of the session is.

Table 4.2

Observing a practitioner working in an area of provision within the Early Years Foundation Stage	
Description of the area of provision (e.g. water/sand/role play area)	Child interactions (non-verbal and verbal)
Information about the children involved (e.g. number, age, sex – is this a new activity for the children or one the children are very familiar with?)	With self
	With others
Focus of the activity	Actions including mark-making, drawing and any other recording included in the activity
What does the practitioner say and do?	
What do the children say and do?	
How does the practitioner monitor the children's achievements? How are children given feedback on their achievements?	
Additional information, e.g. How long did the activity last? What did the children do next? What did the practitioner do next?	

(Continued)

(Continued)

Table 4.3

Prompt sheet for observing an early childhood setting session	
At the beginning of the lesson	
Entry to the session	
Adult activity	Child activity
How does the teacher welcome and direct the children? Are there routine 'beginning' processes, such as going to the mat, returning books, etc.? How is the lesson set out to facilitate the start? Resources used? What do other adults in class do? What does the teacher or other group leader do to direct children? What does the teacher or other group leader do to engage children? Questioning? What does the teacher do if a child is not engaged in an activity? What is the balance of teacher-to-pupil talk? What area of learning do the activities address?	How does the child know what is available? Does the child choose the activity or is the child directed? How does the teacher attract attention? Evidence of pupil's interest and motivation? Does the child interact with other children? What vocabulary does the child use? What resources does the child use? Is there a product, such as drawing, writing, model? What happens to this?
Self-selected activity	
How does the teacher welcome and direct the children? Are there routine 'beginning' processes, such as going to the mat, returning books, etc.? How is the lesson set out to facilitate the start? Resources used? What do other adults in class do? What does the teacher or other group leader do to direct children? What does the teacher or other group leader do to engage children? Questioning? What does the teacher do if a child is not engaged in an activity? What is the balance of teacher-to-pupil talk? What area of learning do the activities address? How does the child know what is available? Does the child choose the activity or is the child directed?	How does the teacher attract attention? Evidence of pupil's interest and motivation? Does the child interact with other children? What vocabulary does the child use? What resources does the child use? Is there a product, such as drawing, writing, model? What happens to this?

Session conclusion	
How does the teacher conclude the lesson?	What is the signal for this phase of the lesson?
What learning does the teacher revisit?	
Which pupils report back on what they have done?	How do pupils arrange their resources?
What vocabulary do pupils use?	Are pupils willing or enthusiastic to recall activities?
How long does this phase of the lesson last?	
How does the teacher manage the transition from seat work to the mat (or group)?	How does the teacher move the group on?

The other key issue you will be involved with is managing the behaviour of the children in your class. This is dealt with later, in much more detail. At the moment, however, the chief priority is to make a good start with this particular group of children. Read the school's behaviour policy as soon as you can and be sure you understand it. Make notes of the key points and check your observations to see what elements of the policy you have already seen in action. Ask your teacher, very early on, what she/he expects from the class, what rules she/he applies and what rewards and sanctions she/he offers. Most teachers are so used to this they may have to think to recall what they actually do but you need to know, so watch and ask. You should set the same standards, enforce the same rules and offer the same rewards as your teacher. To do this you must know what they are!

By the end of your preparation days in school you should know most of the following.

- **What subjects and/or topics are being taught during your time in that class.**
- **The class routine.**
- **The names and broad characteristics of the children in your class, sets or groups.**
- **The school behaviour and health and safety policies and how these are implemented in your class.**
- **The names and roles of staff involved with your children.**
- **The daily routines of the class and school.**
- **Staffroom etiquette.**
- **The location and procedures for resources (in broad terms).**

You should be able to participate in lessons and talk confidently to the children.

Key Stages 1 and 2

For these key stages, you should make:

- **at least one observation of the teacher's behaviour management in a mathematics and an English lesson;**
- **at least one observation of the teacher's behaviour management in a non-core subject lesson;**
- **at least one observation of the teacher's behaviour management outside the classroom, the hall or the IT suite;**

- observations of mathematics, English and science lessons so that you can see the structures of these lessons;
- observations of break time and lunchtime routines for the class.

Early Years Foundation Stage

For this key stage, you should make:

- at least one observation of the teacher's behaviour management in a teacher directed group session;
- at least one observation of the teacher's behaviour management in a child-led session;
- at least one observation of the teacher's behaviour management in the outdoor classroom;
- a focused observation of arrival and departure times and of the changeover time for part-time children – this not only introduces routines but also gives you models of how experienced staff interact with parents;
- focused observation of fruit or drinks times;
- focused observation of story or action rhyme times.

MINI CASE MINI CASE **MINI CASE** **MINI CASE** MINI CASE MINI CASE **MINI CASE**

In my first term I did some observation before I began teaching. I spent four days watching and helping groups. It meant I had seen most of a week and I had a feel for the rhythm of the class and expectations of behaviour. But I felt a bit of a fraud and I was really keen to get on to the teaching. I only had four weeks in that class, after all. I started teaching as soon as I could began and built up to doing whole days in my second week. Looking back, I realise I didn't observe carefully enough at the beginning and now I wish I'd grabbed the opportunity when I had it. As the weeks went on, I kept coming up with quite obvious questions about things like rules and routines that I should have been able to answer. I will be taking the observation part of my time in my next school much more seriously on this placement.

Ann, SCITT PGCE trainee

As I had worked in the school for a year as a TA, I really didn't think I needed to do the observation tasks but my mentor was playing it by the book and made me use observation grids for lessons. It turned out to be really useful, particularly the observation for behaviour management. I found that when I took the class I was actually copying phrases and gestures the teacher used. I don't do that now, but it got me started and established me as a teacher. If I had to offer advice it would be to observe more than one teacher and see how different teachers implement the same policy.

Ellie, SCITT trainee

My final placement was the really important one, because the way my course worked that was the assessed placement. I made sure I did the observations I needed. At the start of that block of teaching I did routine observations of the teacher to learn how to manage the class. I also observed every subject before I taught it for the first time. As the block progressed I used observations to address standards I still had outstanding. I did a really good afternoon observing the EAL teacher when she worked with some children in a group and some in a class. The strategies she used had been discussed in my course, but having the opportunity to see them used brought them alive and gave me ideas for using them in my class. It is hard to observe, because you feel you should be teaching but, as I see it, I might not get the chance when I am an NQT.

Jo, PGCE Early Years

Focused observations

As your time in the class progresses, you will be able to select your observations in a much more purposeful way. You might observe your teacher for the following reasons:

- **You have not had a chance to see a particular type of lesson. You will not want to wait three weeks before beginning your teaching and some subjects will be blocked so that they do not happen every week, or even every term.**
- **You have found a particular difficulty in your teaching and you want to find out how the teacher addresses this (and develop your own confidence). For example, if you are unsure about how to use your voice to gain children's attention or you need some strategies for teaching phonics.**
- **You have an outstanding target to address and observation is the best way of doing this. For instance, if you are aiming to improve your differentiation through questioning, first see how the teacher does it.**

To make the best possible use of these observations of your teacher's practice, make sure you have read any relevant documentation and are well prepared. If you are observing science, you will learn much more if you have read the school science policy and have looked at the relevant part of the Scheme of Work for science. If you have been able to see the planning for the lesson you will learn even more.

In your school based training you will also observe and talk to other teachers in your school because they are a huge resource of expertise.

- **If you are in an Early Years setting you will observe the other members of the team, as the teaching of the group is a shared responsibility.**
- **If you do not have a chance to observe a particular type of teaching in your class your mentor can always arrange for you to go to another class. For instance, if your Key Stage 2 class are doing art but not D&T this term, you can go to another class to observe D&T.**
- **If another class has a particular resource you want to see in use, such as an interactive whiteboard (IWB), parachute or outdoor area, your mentor may help you arrange an observation.**
- **If another teacher in the school has a particular expertise your mentor may well arrange for you to observe them teaching in this area, for instance a particularly good English or mathematics teacher or a computing co-ordinator.**
- **Observing a SENCO is very valuable because you can gain insight into the processes of the SEND code of practice and also see teaching strategies at work.**
- **Observing an EAL teacher or support assistant will help you not only to understand a wide range of strategies, but also to include them in your teaching.**
- **Observing a class outside your key stages will help you to understand the experiences and needs of children in the key stages preceding and following yours. It will help you to think about the demands of transition.**

You need to be prepared to make the most of these observations. If you are going to observe the use of an IWB, review the notes of any training you have had so far. If you are going to talk to the SENCO and observe a group session, make sure you have read the school SEND policy and the IEPs of any children in your class.

Through observation you will learn that there are many different ways to be a successful teacher. On the basis of what you observe, you can start to develop a range of successful strategies. Once you use these strategies yourself they will become part of your personal teaching style.

Sample lesson observation format for Key Stages 1 and 2

The purpose of observing experienced teachers is to examine the range of techniques that the teacher is using in order to reflect on your own practice. You can use the grid in Tables 4.4 and 4.5 to make notes.

Table 4.4

Trainee's name		Teacher observed	Date and time
Class	Lesson topic		
Starting the lesson/transitions within the lesson		Links made to previous learning	
Teaching strategies		Pupil activities	
Organisation of the learning		Use of resources (including use of IT)	
Management of pupils		Strategies for assessing pupil learning	
Consideration of special needs		Teacher presence in the classroom	
Summarising and extending the learning		Concluding the lesson	

Sample lesson observation format for Early Years Foundation Stage

Table 4.5

Description of the area of provision (e.g. water/small world/role-play area)	
Information about the children involved (e.g. number, age, sex – Is this a new activity for the children or one the children are very familiar with?)	
Focus of the activity – EYFS	
What does the practitioner say and do?	What do the children say and do?
How does the practitioner monitor the children's achievements? How are children given feedback on their achievements?	
Additional information, e.g. How long did the activity last? What did the children do next? What did the practitioner do next?	

Planning and differentiation

There is no such thing as a good teacher who cannot plan well. Planning is the basis of good teaching and you have a number of reasons for becoming good at planning. First of all, you have to demonstrate that you meet the Teachers' Standards. Teachers' Standard Part 2, Standard 4 requires that you can 'Plan and teach well structured lessons'. In doing which you will need to:

- **impart knowledge and develop understanding through effective use of lesson time**
- **promote a love of learning and children's intellectual curiosity**
- **set homework and plan other out-of-class activities to consolidate and extend the knowledge and understanding pupils have acquired**

- **reflect systematically on the effectiveness of lessons and approaches to teaching**
- **contribute to the design and provision of an engaging curriculum within the relevant subject area(s).**

To demonstrate these standards you will build your expertise at planning gradually as you progress through your placements.

The theory of planning is relatively straightforward and by the time you arrive for your placement you should know about some of the factors shaping the choice of what children learn and how they learn it.

- **The National Curriculum and personal, social and health education (PSHE) requirements. Together with the (local) RE curriculum these provide much of the content of our curriculum at Key Stages 1 and 2.**

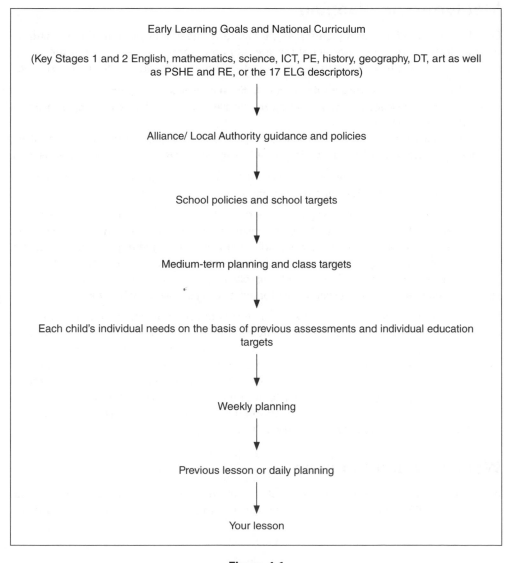

Figure 4.1

- In Early Years Foundation Stage the Early Learning Goals and seven areas of learning stand in the place of a curriculum. This statutory curriculum is supplemented at Early Years Foundation Stage through the curriculum guidance for the Early Years Foundation Stage.
- Academy chains, school alliances or local authorities will offer guidance about teaching and have requirements and policies for the curriculum. These and the school's policies and targets will also shape the material planned for lessons.
- Within school, the curriculum co-ordinators will monitor plans and ensure the curriculum is addressed progressively and continuously.

You need to be involved in different levels of planning during your training. You will have to demonstrate that you know about medium-term planning, especially for English, mathematics, science and ICT at Key Stages 1 and 2, or all seven areas of learning for Early Years Foundation Stage.

Medium-term planning

Drawing up a medium-term plan for, say, a half term means dividing up the learning for the half term so that it can be taught in a continuous, progressive way that meets the needs of all the learners in the class. This is not as simple as it sounds. To do it you need:

- good knowledge of the curriculum documents (National Curriculum, EYFS, etc.);
- good subject knowledge so that you can make sensible divisions and links between elements of knowledge and skill;
- an understanding of how you will teach the subjects and what the pupils' likely responses will be;
- some experience or knowledge of how long it will take for children to learn each element of your plan.

These require some experience, so medium-term planning is usually the first type of planning you see but the last type of planning you actually do.

You may find it difficult to obtain experience of medium-term planning on school based training because teachers in school do this sort of planning well in advance and often refer to last year's plans. Also teachers may not work individually on medium-term planning, but do it in planning teams involving all the teachers teaching the same year group or key stage. It is quite usual for curriculum co-ordinators to work with planning teams or check their plans for a particular subject to ensure that the curriculum for that subject is covered effectively.

Medium-term plans are usually expressed in terms of broad objectives for what the children should learn and these are specifically referenced to (or copied from) the National Curriculum programmes of study, or the Early Years Foundation Stage curriculum. To demonstrate that you know about medium-term planning you should meet with your teacher specifically to discuss planning using the guidance suggested in the practical task below. If you have the opportunity to attend a medium-term planning meeting, you should seize the chance as it will give you the best possible training. This is an opportunity your mentor may be able to arrange for you.

Weekly or unit planning

A weekly plan, or plan for a sequence of lessons over a longer period, is constructed from the medium-term plan. It is more specific than a medium-term plan and will include not only the learning objectives but also the teaching activities, resources and assessment points of the lessons in the sequence. Teachers will usually have a weekly plan for each subject at Key Stages 1 and 2, although there will often be strong links across the curriculum.

In the Early Years Foundation Stage, the plan for a week, or unit of work, will usually be written by at least the teacher and teaching assistant. It may involve a larger team. It will address all the areas of development and will usually be planned around a theme such as summer, the seaside, Diwali, growing, myself, etc. This is to emphasise the links between different areas of development and ensure the learning makes sense to very young children.

There is no one correct format for weekly or unit plans. Most schools have at least one set format that they use for planning but many have different formats for different key stages or even different formats for different subjects. This is especially true in the case of literacy and mathematics at Key Stages 1 and 2, where the structures of the lessons may demand different planning grids. Weekly plans will be referenced to the relevant curriculum documents and will break down learning and teaching so that children can achieve the learning objectives. This is a difficult skill because, as well as everything necessary for medium-term planning, you need to know:

- **what children have already done, know and can do;**
- **the likely response of children to what you are planning;**
- **the pace at which children can work;**
- **any individual needs that demand differentiation at a weekly planning level.**

Example forms for planning a sequence of lessons

Experienced teachers in some schools will teach from their weekly or unit plans. At the start of your training in each school you work in you will not be able, or ready, to do this. You will use the teacher's weekly plans right from the start as guidance so that you know what to expect from lessons or sessions you are observing. By looking at weekly plans you can at least be sure what the learning objective of the lesson is and how you should support children in achieving it. When you start teaching you will plan your early lessons and parts of lessons on the basis of the teacher's weekly plans.

As your school based training progresses, you will be required to write weekly plans (or sequences of lesson plans) for core subjects if you are a Primary trainee or across the seven areas of learning of the Early Learning Goals if you are an Early Years trainee. This does not mean that you will have to do this unsupported. You will seek careful advice about your first weekly plan and use the teacher's medium-term plans as a basis for writing weekly plans. If weekly planning is done as a year group, setting or phase team activity you will be able to do your weekly planning this way but you will be expected to make a significant contribution and to lead the planning at this level before you can achieve the Standards for QTS.

Table 4.6

Sequence of lessons   Term/Year   Teaching group

Curriculum subject/Theme/Area(s) of learning					
(This derives from the school's medium plans)					
Broad learning objectives Specific references to Early Learning Goals, NC, Agreed Syllabus for RE	**Focused learning objectives** Attitudes, skills, knowledge and understanding	**Key activities**	**Resources**	**Cross-curricular aspects**	**Planned method of assessment**
Broad learning objectives	Learning objectives stating anticipated achievement in one or more of the following: • attitudes (show...) • skills (be able to...) • knowledge (know that...) • understanding (develop concept of...) These form the basis of assessment and are judged through planned outcomes.	Activities should: • enable learning objectives to be met • include a variety of experiences that progressively develop children's learning • recognise pupils' diverse needs (including pupils with SEND, and pupils with EAL) • take account of pupils' gender and ethnicity	Resources should be: • influenced by learning objectives • listed in detail • considered with health and safety in mind • related to displays • where relevant	Opportunities to develop significant and planned attitudes, skills, knowledge and understanding across the curriculum in (e.g.): • English • Computing • PSHE • other subjects/areas of learning where significant	Anticipated evidence • to demonstrate achievement of learning objectives, and to inform assessment and record keeping (may be observational, verbal, written or graphic evidence, depending on activity) • to reflect a range of assessment methods

PRACTICAL TASK PRACTICAL TASK PRACTICAL TASK PRACTICAL TASK PRACTICAL TASK

Obtain your teacher's medium-term plans as soon as possible (usually in the first few days). Examine them carefully and ensure you know the following:

- **What period of time does each part of the plan cover? What period of time does the plan cover in total?**

- **For Key Stages 1 or 2 what parts of the National Curriculum, Schemes of Work for the Foundation subjects, PSHE curriculum, and RE syllabus does this medium-term plan address? Make sure you look up all these elements and read them in detail because you do need to demonstrate familiarity with these documents.**

- **For Early Years Foundation Stage, what literacy and mathematics outcomes and areas of learning and development does this medium-term plan address? Make sure you look up all these elements and read them in detail because you do need to demonstrate familiarity with these documents.**

This part of the task will take you at least an hour or so and should be done before you go on to the weekly plan.

Ask your teacher for his or her weekly plans for one of the weeks included in the medium-term plan. Ensure you can answer the following:

- **Which parts of the medium-term plan does the weekly plan address?**

- **Which parts of the relevant curriculum documents does this refer to? (You will be able to see this if you have done the first part of the task well.)**

- **How long will each lesson or session in the weekly plan be?**

- **What additional detail does a weekly plan contain that a medium-term plan does not?**

If you are on placement in Key Stages 1 or 2, you can now focus on one part of the weekly plan, perhaps mathematics, or science. If you are in Early Years Foundation Stage you need to look at all the areas of learning.

- **What resources are needed for the lessons in the weekly plan?**

- **Who will be teaching the lessons in the weekly plan? Are they for a particular set or area of learning?**

Discuss your chosen element of weekly planning with your teacher. You should ask:

- **How do you derive a weekly plan from the medium-term plan?**

- **What do you do if the children do not make the predicted learning gains in one week?**

- **How do you ensure that the learning is accessible to all the children in the class?**

- **How do you differentiate for children who have SEN, EAL or are in the gifted and talented register?**

- **Please can you show me how you include children with SEND or individualised targets?**

Lesson or session planning

A lesson or session plan is written from a weekly (or longer-term) plan. It is a detailed document that addresses every element of the lesson/session. For you this has two main purposes.

First, a lesson plan enables you to demonstrate that you can select the appropriate objectives, teaching methods, assessment points and resources to teach an interesting, relevant and successful lesson. Lesson plans serve to show that you can identify children's learning and to lead on to the next teaching experience. Secondly, writing lesson plans is a formative experience that gives you the chance to rehearse lessons before you do them. In this way you learn to deliver the content you mean to deliver. You also learn to manage challenging aspects of teaching such as pace, questioning, class management and enthusiasm. By planning lessons carefully in writing, you will gradually develop the mental scripts for teaching, assessment and class management that experienced teachers have so that, eventually, you no longer need to write lesson plans. At the beginning of every placement you will be expected to write lesson/session plans for every lesson or session you teach but later in the placement your mentor may suggest you no longer need to do this. If this happens you may teach from weekly plans.

There is no perfect lesson plan format but lesson plans need to include most of the following.

- **Class/group taught.**
- **Time and duration of lesson.**
- **Learning objective(s). This is the most important point on the plan. What do you want the children to learn, understand or do as a result of your lesson? Think very carefully about expressing lesson objectives so that they are reasonable and achievable. A single session or lesson may address or contribute to a literacy or mathematics objective or to an EYFS area of learning but no lesson will cover one of these big objectives. You may want to reference them on your lesson plan but phrase your lesson objective accurately so that the children can achieve it.**
- **Reference to the relevant curriculum documentation (NC, EYFS, schemes of work, etc.).**
- **The structure of the session. Does the lesson have a three-part structure? Most lessons have an introduction, main body and a plenary. A mathematics lesson might have a mental/oral starter, a main activity and a plenary. An English lesson might have a shared part, a main activity and a plenary. In Early Years Foundation Stage is there a teacher-led then child-selected activity? Do nursery children do a plan/do/review format?**
- **The timings of each part of the lesson.**
- **Key vocabulary to be used.**
- **Key questions to be asked.**
- **Key teaching points.**
- **Role of the teacher and teaching assistants.**
- **Learning activity (what the children do).**
- **List of resources and use of outdoor classroom (for Early Years Foundation Stage).**
- **Identified outcomes (how will you assess whether the children have achieved their learning objective?).**
- **Note of pupils' previous experience.**
- **Cross-curricular links.**
- **Use of ICT.**
- **Identified health and safety issues (such as glue guns, the need to wear coats, etc.).**
- **An evaluation section.**

Here are some examples of lesson plans and formats. No format is perfect but any of these can be adapted and changed. Your course tutor or mentor will probably suggest a format you might use. Your mentor will certainly, at some point in your school based training, suggest that you adapt your lesson plan format to help you address a particular target. For example:

- **If you are finding it difficult to maintain the pace of a lesson, you may want to plan in five minute intervals and note down the times at the side of your lesson plans.**
- **If you are having difficulty focusing on key vocabulary, you may want to highlight or embolden this in your plan.**
- **If preparation is a particular target, you may need to list resources especially carefully.**
- **If moving the children around the classroom is an issue for you, you may want to plan transitions very carefully.**

Your lesson plans could well change format for a short time to assist you in addressing your target.

Generic lesson plan to adapt for specific subjects (Key Stages 1 and 2)

Table 4.7

Date	Class/year group or set including number of pupils
Pupils' previous experience	
Notes from previous lesson including errors and misconceptions that need to addressed in this lesson	
NC references or, where appropriate, the relationship with the school's scheme of work	Learning objectives
Cross-curricular focus: spiritual, social, cultural, moral	

(Continued)

Table 4.7   (Continued)

Particular Teachers' Standards to focus on for observation	
Resources for each phase of the lesson	Subject-specific language
Specific expectations for behaviour (make clear to pupils)	
Appropriate speaking and listening objectives. Planned links, where appropriate, to English and/or mathematics for all subjects	

Mental/oral starter or other introductory activity (Time) Assessment Activity and questions to ask: Can the pupils?	
Introduction to the main activity (Time) Teacher	Pupils

Main activity (Time) Phase Assessment: Can the pupils?	Low attainers Extension/challenge	Middle attainers Extension/challenge	High attainers Extension/challenge

Teacher's role during the main activity

Differentiation/target-setting including individual targets where appropriate	Use of in-class support, including guidance to supporting adult(s)

Plenary (Time)

Key questions to ask/areas to discuss

Introduce homework where appropriate

Note any errors/misconceptions to focus on in the next lesson on this area.

Evaluation of the lesson

Annotate the plan, using a different colour. Add other working notes here. After the session make any relevant notes that will help you to support pupils' progression/plan a similar session. This may include references to specific pupils (which may or may not need to go on their records)/ ideas to reinforce the learning/suggestions for alternative organisational strategies/comments on the appropriateness of the resources.

Focus on pupils' learning

Pupils not reaching the objectives, how and why?	Pupils exceeding the objectives, how and why?

Notes for next lesson focusing on teaching

Good aspects of teaching	Areas for development

Generic lesson plan to adapt for Early Years Foundation Stage areas of learning

Table 4.8

Focus of the activity
Children involved (e.g. number, age, sex – Is this a new activity for the children or one the children are very familiar with?) Self-selection? Practitioner-directed?
Resources/Description of the area of provision (e.g. water/small world/role-play area)

Key practitioner vocabulary and questions?	What do the children say and do?
Evidence of achievement	Interaction with others?
Observations of participants	Action for future activity

Your very first plans

Your very first plans will probably not be for whole lessons or sessions. Initially, you will plan for short parts of lessons or sessions such as the mental/oral starter in a mathematics lesson, a guided reading session for a small group of children, supervision of an outdoor activity or a whole class phonics game. In planning these parts of lessons you will have the chance to pay attention to detail and really concentrate on some important aspects of using plans such as:

- **ensuring you say what you plan to say;**
- **maintaining a pace that is brisk and engaging but not so fast that the children are lost;**
- **questioning and interactive teaching.**

Planning parts of lessons and teaching them is a good start to building up responsibility for whole lessons. Initially, you will want to ask your teacher to look at your plans and make suggestions. In this way you are more likely to pitch the activity at the right level for the children. This is a skilled exercise that demands some experience of the children and their previous work. When going into a new class you will need the support of the class teacher to pitch the activities at the right level.

Planner for a mental/oral starter

Table 4.9

Date	Group/class	
Duration	NC for literacy and mathematics reference	
Resources	Mathematical, literacy, etc., language	
Activity		
Questions		
Less confident	Confident	More confident

(Continued)

Table 4.9   (Continued)

Assessment		
Less confident	Confident	More confident

Evaluation

Planning for other adults in the class or setting

As your school based training progresses, you will develop expertise and speed in your planning. You will plan for a wider range of subjects and a wider range of situations. One key issue you need to consider, as you assume a greater role in planning for the class and as soon as you are planning whole class lessons, is planning for teaching assistants. It is usual for teachers to teach with teaching assistants and to plan for them.

A planning format for a teaching assistant

Table 4.10

Date.................................   Lesson focus...

Activity (a brief account of the activity and the TA's role in any whole class introduction, shared reading, phonics groups, etc.)
Equipment needed
Key vocabulary to use
Key questions to use

For completion by the TA after group work

Table 4.11

Names	Objectives	can do	needs help	notes
	1			
	2			
	3			
	1			
	2			
	3			
	1			
	2			
	3			
	1			
	2			
	3			
	1			
	2			
	3			

In the Early Years Foundation Stage, practitioners will probably use the same planning sheets as the teacher and will make evaluations and assessments like the teacher. In Key Stages 1 and 2 there is a wider variety of practice. To ensure you work well with the teaching assistant, we suggest you use a set format to present clear expectations of what you would like the teaching assistant to do. You should also leave a space for the TA to write assessment notes about how well the children achieved the objective. These notes may well affect your future planning.

Frequently asked questions

1. **'I have been planning my lessons on the computer every night. It is taking me hours and hours to type them up and I am becoming very tired. What can I do?'**

Your priority is clear, accessible, useful plans and it does not matter whether they are written or word processed. If writing by hand works better for you, then write the plans by hand. If it worries you, you can always word process plans for the sessions when your mentor or course tutor is observing you. This has the added bonus of showing that you are making an effort to assist the observer and you will gain points for taking a professional approach. Of course, you may find that the computer is faster if you are adapting internet plans.

2. **'I have found loads of plans on the internet but my teacher says I can't just print these off and use them. Why not?'**

There are hundreds of lesson plans available on sites like the Times Educational Supplement (http://www.tes.co.uk/article.aspx?storycode=6081306&s_cid=Landing_LessonPlans12), or the Hamilton Trust site (https://www.hamilton-trust.org.uk/). There is nothing wrong with these plans except that they are not necessarily right for your situation. To use them you must adapt them to the needs and prior experience of your children as well as the weekly or medium-term planning for your class. Once a unit of work is started, each group of children will work through at a different rate and no plans created at a distance can accommodate this. If you can adapt plans from the internet to meet the needs of your children and the pace of your planning, they may work very well for you. Most trainees use adapted, internet-based plans some of the time, but many say they find it is just as quick to start from scratch. However, you cannot have too many ideas and internet plans are ideal for generating ideas.

3. **'I am doing school based training in an Early Years Foundation Stage unit and the staff are used to planning together as a team on a weekly basis. Each member of staff plans one or two areas of the curriculum. How can I get involved and get the right experience?'**

This is a common situation and your mentor will have ways to involve you. You might start by creating more detailed session plans from the team's weekly plans for each area of learning you work in. This will help you to focus on the details of sessions such as key language, interaction with children and observation. As the training progresses you will take a larger role in planning meetings and by the end of your block of training in this unit you should be able to make helpful suggestions towards the weekly plan. Remember to do (and plan) the routine aspects of teaching at Early Years Foundation Stage that the team may not plan. These include reading to children regularly, managing fruit time, helping children to change books and take home books and story sacks, managing the home time routine and welcome, and modelling writing. Plan these sessions carefully.

4. **'I write my lesson plans out in proper sentences but my friend uses note form. Who is right?'**

Probably both of you are right. If note form is quicker and still includes detail it is a good working compromise. You can write in more detail when you know the lesson plan will be the object of scrutiny, such as for an observation by your mentor.

5. **'I have planned and taught lessons for English, mathematics, computing and science (and other subjects) and now my mentor is asking me to do sequences of lessons. She insists I should do sequences in the core subjects but I'd rather do sequences in art and music. Can she insist?'**

Yes – she has your training interests at heart. To meet the Teachers' Standards you must demonstrate you can plan lessons and sequences of lessons in the core subjects and others. A different level of planning is required for planning across the non-core subjects at Key Stages 1 and 2. You must be able to plan other subject lessons from the teacher's medium-term plans, with teacher support. This is a rather less demanding level of planning. Your mentor is making sure you use your school based training time to focus on the planning that will enable you to meet the standards.

Evaluation

Planning goes hand in hand with evaluation. To demonstrate your ability to be self-critical (Preamble to Teachers' Standards) you need to be able to improve your performance through self-evaluation. This is discussed in more detail in the next chapter but cannot go unmentioned here. Evaluation means considering:

- **how well the children achieved your objectives and made learning progress;**
- **how well you planned, taught and managed teaching in relation to your targets.**

You will be required to include evaluations on most of your lesson plans and you will see spaces for these in the lesson plan formats provided. Evaluations will usually be brief and will usually focus on two aspects: what the children learned and what you did.

If every time you taught a lesson you wrote a detailed critique of your performance as a teacher, linked to The Standards, you would never have time to teach. Perhaps this is why some trainees start every evaluation they write with the dreaded sentence 'The lesson went well'. This is an ineffective evaluation because it tells the reader nothing except that the trainee survived to teach again. What went well? Does 'well' mean the children learned something?

It is much more useful to focus on particular aspects of your teaching to evaluate and improve. This is the role of the targets that are discussed in later chapters. For example, if you are really concentrating on managing the class, then you need to monitor how successful you are at managing behaviour, what strategies worked and what progress you are making. If you have this sort of evaluation for a series of lessons you can decide when you have achieved this target and when it is time to identify a new target.

Many trainee teachers strike a balance between in-depth evaluation and time saving by annotating lesson plans with evaluations and doing only one detailed critique of a lesson each week and a weekly evaluation. If you annotate lesson plans, it is important to realise you will need to make comments about pupil learning and your teaching, but you will also need to cross out and amend the objectives of subsequent lessons, depending on pupil learning. Your mentor and tutor will be interested in your annotations, because they show you adapt your planning in response to pupil learning. It would be a waste of time, and a missed opportunity to show your use of evaluations, to type up such annotations.

When you begin planning and teaching you will probably be very keen to hear positive evaluations but less keen to hear advice on improvement. However, you should develop your ability to listen to advice and act on it. A key feature of the resilience discussed in Chapter 1 is the ability to accept limitations and look to future experiences positively. Your teacher will be in a good position to obtain a wide ranging view of your performance and will help you to evaluate in a critical but positive way.

When your evaluation comment identifies an improvement you can make, always say what you propose to do in response. The very best planning is the sort that clearly uses evidence from children's previous attainment and leads on to influence the planning and teaching of the next session or lesson. This sort of evidence may be the annotations to a lesson plan you make in response to previous evaluations.

Differentiation

In order to meet the diverse learning needs of pupils, teachers aim to teach the knowledge, skills and understanding in ways that suit their pupils' abilities – this is called differentiation. You must demonstrate your ability to do this in order to meet Teachers' Standards, Part One, Standard 6 'Make accurate and productive use of assessment'. All teachers should set high expectations and provide opportunities for all children to achieve including:

- **boys and girls;**
- **children with special educational needs;**
- **children with disabilities;**
- **children from all social and cultural backgrounds;**

- children of different ethnic groups including travellers, refugees and asylum seekers;
- children from diverse linguistic backgrounds.

Differentiation is represented in different forms in your planning, and involves:

- **Presentation** – planning to use a variety of media to present ideas, offering vocabulary or extra diagrams to those who need more support. Writing grids might be a form of presentation to help young writers who need extra support, where more confident writers do not have such support.
- **Content** – selecting appropriately so that there is content that suits most children with additional content available to some. This might mean some children completing six calculations where others complete ten.
- **Resources** – use resources that support pupils' needs such as writing frame, language master word banks or spellmaster machines for poor spellers. For children with EAL you might need to ensure that target vocabulary is available in a written form.
- **Grouping** – grouping pupils of similar ability for targeted support or pairing with a more able pupil, teaching assistant or language support teacher.
- **Task** – matching tasks to pupils' abilities. This can mean different tasks for different pupils. It is sometimes a good idea to offer different tasks that address the same objectives to different pupils so that they can achieve success.
- **Support** – offering additional adult or peer assistance, from a teaching assistant, language support teacher or more experienced child.
- **Time** – giving more or less time to complete a given task can make the task more suitable to the particular pupils.

As you develop your planning you will need to be sure to address the needs of all children. To do this you will plan different activities, support, resources, content, time and presentation so that all the children can achieve the learning objectives. Although this sounds simple it demands really good knowledge of the content, the children and a range of teaching strategies. At first you may well over- or underestimate what children know and can do. You will only achieve appropriate differentiation by working closely with the teacher so that you find out what strategies are available and which work for these children. Key resources will be teaching assistants, language support staff and individualised targets written for children with special needs. All these should be planned into your lessons.

REFLECTIVE TASK

Review your early plans for:

- a whole class session;
- a group activity;
- an individual task to be used with a larger group or class of children.

Focus on your use of questioning in each of these situations.

How have you differentiated the task to meet the needs of individuals?

Ensure you have considered:

- who you will question;
- the function of the questions (bringing to mind knowledge, checking, keeping order, etc.);

- **how you will phrase questions and what key vocabulary you will use;**
- **what sorts of answers you are looking for.**

Questioning is a key area for differentiation.

A SUMMARY OF KEY POINTS

- Observation is the first step towards teaching. You will need to observe at the start of your school based training and later in the term, or placement. Do not teach a subject you have not observed. Observation is also a tool for increasing your knowledge and experience. Choose your observations to meet your training needs.

- Planning is the foundation of good teaching and learning. Careful planning will help you to teach the right content, manage the class, maintain a good pace, give children feedback and assess learning.

- You will encounter medium-term planning for a half term, weekly planning and short-term, lesson or session planning.

- Begin planning small elements of sessions and build up to whole sessions. When you can plan lessons build up to sequences of lessons or core subject lessons.

- Planning is often done in teams. You will be planning with the support of your teacher and, possibly, a wider teaching team.

- Seize any opportunity to be involved in medium-term planning and to attend planning meetings.

- Differentiate your plans so that all children are included and plan for teaching assistants and other practitioners.

- Evaluation is your tool for ensuring learning takes place – in yourself and the children. Evaluate lessons and sequences of lessons.

RESOURCES RESOURCES **RESOURCES** RESOURCES RESOURCES **RESOURCES**

The National Curriculum is the starting point for most of the planning you will do. https://www.gov.uk/government/collections/national-curriculum

The *Times Educational Supplement* New Teachers site has a number of useful guides to lesson planning. http://newteachers.tes.co.uk/news/realistic-guide-lesson-planning/45965

One of the most comprehensive collections of lesson plans and ideas is the Primary Resources site. http://www.primaryresources.co.uk/

5
Learning to teach in school based training

Learning outcomes

By the end of this chapter you should:

- **know how to build up your teaching as your school based training progresses;**
- **know some of the features of interactive teaching;**
- **know how to set homework;**
- **recognise opportunities to play a wider role in school;**
- **understand the role of school-based tasks in building up your experience.**

Teaching

Surprisingly, many trainees find teaching a class or group is less challenging than planning and assessing. You can aim to demonstrate that you meet all the teaching standards (Teachers' Standards, Part One, pp.13–14):

1 **Set high expectations which inspire, motivate and challenge pupils**
2 **Promote good progress and outcomes by pupils**
3 **Demonstrate good subject and curriculum knowledge**
4 **Plan and teach well structured lessons**
5 **Adapt teaching to respond to the strengths and needs of all pupils**
6 **Make accurate and productive use of assessment**
7 **Manage behaviour effectively to ensure a good and safe learning environment**
8 **Fulfil wider professional responsibilities.**

To tackle this daunting list of standards you should aim to build up your teaching gradually. Start by planning and teaching small parts of lessons, based on the class teacher's plans and using strategies you have seen the teacher using. This might mean you start in a Foundation Key Stage class by planning and managing a small word activity or a dramatic play area and work to interact effectively with children who choose to do that activity. In a Key Stage 1 class you might start out by doing a whole-class mental/oral starter in mathematics or a shared reading session in English. In Key Stage 2 you might start by taking a group guided reading session or using the interactive whiteboard to introduce a whole-class activity in mathematics or literacy.

You will move on to teaching complete lessons with the support of the teacher, who will help you to establish yourself as a teacher, to maintain a purposeful working environment and to teach the appropriate material. As you develop confidence, a suitable relationship with the children and a range of strategies for teaching, you will plan and teach a wide range of lessons or sessions, increasing the range of strategies for differentiation and ensuring all the children's needs are met. Eventually, you will plan and teach sequences of lessons that take the children through a process of learning about a topic or set of skills. This process of building up your level of responsibility and range of teaching techniques is different for each trainee because your experience is unique and each class of children is different. We asked seven NQTs for their top tips for beginner teachers and this is what they suggested:

Know what you are talking about

You must be absolutely clear about what you are teaching so that you can introduce the topic clearly to the children and understand and address their errors and misconceptions. No one else can do this for you and if you do not have the necessary subject knowledge you may teach the wrong content or be unable to help children. You need to be able to think flexibly about the topic so that you can understand children's errors and misconceptions. This means knowing the topic well. Always research your lessons so that you can demonstrate good subject and curriculum knowledge (Teaching Standard 3) and check the relevant curriculum documentation.

Prepare your resources well in advance

If you do not do this, something is bound to come up. As a trainee teacher it will be harder for you to locate resources or have them produced, because you do not know the system. If you leave organising your resources until just before a session things are certain to go wrong (the copier will jam, the corn flour will go missing or there will be no blue paint). You will become flustered and this will unsettle the children.

Put up your objectives and discuss them

If you just write objectives up on the whiteboard for Key Stages 1 and 2 children, the objectives will become so much classroom wallpaper. If you just discuss objectives, some children will forget them. If you write them up, hold them up and discuss what they mean, there is a good chance that both you and the children will understand them.

Explain very clearly

Explain then check whether the children have understood you. Every teacher will be able to tell you about times when they have not said what they meant and have been faced with baffled children. Most children will answer 'yes' to the question 'Do you understand what you have to do?', so avoid this question. Say: 'Tell me what you are going to do'. Occasionally, you will find that they do not know and this will usually be because you have missed out a vital point. Try using little cards with key words to remind yourself of the points you have to explain.

Act as if you know the rules, rewards and sanctions

This will give you confidence: if you act as if you do not know the rules you will lose credibility in the eyes of your class. Even the youngest Early Years Foundation Stage child can spot someone who does not know what they are doing. If you are unsure, you can always ask a child but ask in a way that suggests confidence: 'Right, now show me where you keep your book. Well done!' is better than giving an indication that you do not know what to do.

Keep children moving and keep them involved

If your questioning involves a whole range of children and demands that they do something in response to questions, they are much more likely to engage with the activity. In the later section on questioning there is more advice on this. Even a little movement can make an activity more memorable and purposeful for children. For instance, ask children to perform action rhymes, not just recite them. Get them to stand up and sit down as they answer a rapid-fire tables test. These are small, important things but they can have a surprisingly positive effect.

Keep up the pace

Pace the lesson so that you maintain the children's engagement and fit your plenary in. The plenary is a very important part of a session. Your can restate the teaching points, monitor who has understood and take the learning forward in a very brief plenary. Even at Early Years Foundation Stage, children learn from a brief reflection. Maintaining pace is a real challenge when you begin teaching.

Ham it up

Use your voice, body and other visual aids in an exaggerated way to generate enthusiasm, interest and motivation.

Get to know the children and their abilities quickly

This is a counsel of perfection and you will find it very challenging. However, the sooner you have a broad understanding of children's current abilities and past experience, the sooner your lessons will go smoothly. When working with a new class, most teachers and trainees experience lessons that turn out to be unexpectedly short or long. Until you know the class you are not able to match the work to the children's needs. Meanwhile, check with your teacher often and get him or her to check lesson plans.

Give prompt, balanced feedback

Whether this is about knowledge, skills or behaviour, the most important thing is that you notice and respond. Generally, a small, positive response such as a nod, smile or 'Well done' is all that is required. Do not praise effusively – this devalues the currency. Remember that the children who need the feedback most are often those who are least able to wait for it.

Do not panic – ever

You are in control for as long as you stay calm and are enjoying your work. If you panic you will lose control and find yourself acting unwisely.

Questioning and interactive teaching

Questioning and interactive teaching are vital aspects of Early Years or Primary teaching. You will need to be able to adapt your language to suit the learners you teach, introducing new ideas and concepts clearly, and use explanations, questions, and discussion effectively.

Interactive teaching involves a powerful set of strategies to ensure children learn in ways that suit them best. It is also a very powerful ally for behaviour management. Children who are interested, involved and engaged with an activity are easy to manage.

Questioning

Optimise the interaction between you and your pupils by ensuring that your questioning is as effective as possible. Questioning, either by the teacher or among the children, is a crucial part of introducing a topic and effective at the end of the lesson. It allows you to

- **identify what children already know;**
- **engage them in finding out more;**
- **explore misconceptions and errors;**
- **theorise aloud about new ideas;**
- **demonstrate new learning.**

There are a number of types of questions:

- **closed questions have one clear answer (e.g. 'How much is two add one?');**
- **open questions have open-ended answers (e.g. 'How does the cornflour feel?');**
- **product questions are designed to find the answer to a particular problem;**
- **process questions are meant to elicit procedures, processes and rules used to get the answers.**

The mix of question types you use will depend on the objectives of the session. Your teaching is likely to be more effective if you use more open than closed questions, and more process than product questions. It is very easy to maintain a brisk pace with low-level closed questions but this does not ensure the best learning.

How long you wait for answers depends on the type of question asked. Allow three seconds or so for a lower level factual recall question, and 10–15 seconds for higher level questions (those requiring more sophisticated thinking skills). This will seem a very long wait indeed, but avoid the temptation to fill the space with talk. After the waiting time has passed you should prompt the children. If you ask a complex question requiring a lot of thought, allow children some time to work the answer out on their own – this is where talk partners or the use of small whiteboards are invaluable. You will sometimes want to ask specific individuals in a questioning session and this can be a valuable part of your differentiation or assessment.

Getting some children, especially shy children, to answer a question can be problematic. Give children plenty of experience of interactive lessons, and create a positive atmosphere in which the risks of a wrong answer are bearable. Children are more likely to be involved if they feel confident that a wrong response will not elicit criticism or ridicule from you or other children.

Prompting can be useful to help children answer questions. There are three kinds of prompts:

- **verbal prompts:** these include cues, reminders, instructions, tips, references to previous lessons, or giving part sentences for children to complete;
- **gestural prompts:** the teacher models the behaviour of children in order to pre-empt any mistake, e.g. by pointing to the object they want a child to use, or showing how to hold a pen correctly;
- **physical prompts:** these may be necessary among young learners, e.g. if the child cannot yet hold a crayon or form letters or numbers, you can take their hand and guide them.

Vary your acknowledgement of a child's response according to the confidence with which they gave it: a correct, quick and firm response must be acknowledged in a business-like way (a nod or a gesture), although lower ability and less self-confident children may need more praise. When a child answers a question correctly but hesitantly, give them more explicit feedback to reassure them that the answer was correct and help them remember the correct response. If several of the children seem hesitant you may be asking questions that they do not understand and may need to backtrack to make sure they are with you.

There are two types of wrong answers – those due to carelessness or lack of effort, and those due to a lack of understanding or knowledge. In both cases you need to show that the answer is wrong in a business-like way without resorting to personal criticism. If an answer shows carelessness or lack of effort, move on quickly to the next child – the denial of possible praise is the best response to a lazy answer. Where there is lack of understanding or knowledge, prompt the child by simplifying the question (perhaps breaking it into a series of small steps) or hinting. If this fails, look to the next respondent for the correct answer, rather than giving it yourself. If a child gives a partly right answer, first make clear the part that is correct and the part that is not, to avoid confusing the child or the class. Then prompt the child to correct the incorrect part of the answer. If this does not work, ask another child to correct or develop the part-answer.

PRACTICAL TASK PRACTICAL TASK PRACTICAL TASK PRACTICAL TASK PRACTICAL TASK

Focus on your questioning. A really simple practical task you can do with your teacher is to ask him or her to observe a session where you question a group of children. For each box the observer should tick the type of question you asked and whether you asked a boy or girl.

Table 5.1

Question type	Gender of child asked
Open	Boy
Closed	Girl

Discuss the results of this and consider whether you need to monitor the balance of your questioning.

Interactive teaching

Interactive teaching is simply varying your teaching so that it engages the maximum number of children. Interactive teaching enables you to address children's learning through different sensory channels and to elicit responses from as many children as possible. This means you can make assessments of more children.

Teachers in schools are currently concerned that children learn through a number of sensory channels: visual, auditory and kinaesthetic. Traditionally, we teach relying heavily on the auditory channel by telling children and expecting them to listen. However, it has been suggested that teachers should use more visual learning (based on looking) and more active, kinaesthetic learning. This sounds sensible – there are many ways to learn and as teachers we need to find approaches which best suit our pupils. Do not be taken in, however, by suggestions that different children have different 'learning styles'. Although this idea has become popular there is, in fact, no research evidence at all that such 'learning styles' have any psychological reality. The way something is best learnt may depend on what it is and it would be wrong to label children as 'visual learners' or 'auditory learners' when all children need to learn to use all the channels.

Whenever you are talking to or questioning a group of children, ensure that as many as possible are engaged with you, are responding and are active. Use:

- **small whiteboards on which answers can be written;**
- **talk partners, where children discuss a proposition in pairs for 20 seconds before responding;**
- **phonic or number fans to indicate responses;**
- **picture sorting cards and artefacts that can be held up in response to questions.**

These strategies not only allow you to see at a glance how a wider range of children respond but they give children response time and activity, as well as visual cues.

Also consider how you can make even the simplest activity more active. For instance:

- **if you are teaching children to sing the alphabet, give each child a letter card and play 'stand up' so that they have to stand up when their letter name is sung;**
- **use large PE hoops for sorting activities rather than small ones;**
- **do active phonics games or action counting rhymes daily;**
- **when you ask children to identify something in a whole-class lesson, get them to come out and show the others on the whiteboard, interactive whiteboard or text;**
- **look for opportunities in the outdoor classroom – placing objects on a large alphabet mat is a much more engaging phonic activity than doing a worksheet;**
- **act out action rhymes rather than simply singing them;**
- **use active mathematics games for the lesson starter.**

You can also make learning more visual by asking children to represent thoughts in a variety of different ways – mind maps, grids, arrangements of objects, collections of digital photos and PowerPoint shows.

Frequently asked questions

1. **'My first school did whole-class English lessons including phonics and guided reading groups, with big writing on Fridays. But my second school does something completely different. The phonics is done separately and my teacher does not do guided reading.'**

There are lots of different ways of addressing the teaching of English. Schools vary considerably in the ways they address this vital curriculum component. You should make sure you understand the way phonics is taught in your school and take part in teaching it, in or outside of a dedicated English lesson. Some schools set for phonics right across Reception, Year 1 and Year 2. You can do a check to see that all the elements of effective literacy teaching are being done. Ask your teacher how she or he ensures the children study a wide range of texts, or how the children practise sustained writing. If you are still concerned, discuss this with your mentor.

2. **'I have been observing and working with groups and my mentor wants me to teach the whole class. I am nervous. Help!'**

It sounds as if you have reached a point where you need to take a deep breath, plan carefully and – have a go. It is vital to teach the whole class, if only for short bursts like the introduction to a lesson or a concluding plenary, initially. If you cannot do this you cannot be a teacher. You should teach the whole class quite early in your school based training because the longer you leave it, the harder it is to begin and the harder it is to establish your role in the minds of the children. Review your observations, plan your first attempts carefully and check plans with the teacher. Do not expect everything to be perfect first time.

3. **'In my Foundation Stage unit, I don't have the chance to teach the whole class at once. Is this a problem?'**

No, your unit probably does not use this organisation for sound educational reasons. Discuss these with your teacher or mentor and try to understand why a whole-class grouping is not helpful here.

4. **'I did my first science lesson yesterday and it was a disaster. I couldn't keep my eyes on all the children and some were rude and noisy. This was a lesson plan from my course. What am I doing wrong? Will I ever recover?'**

Move on – but do not forget the experience. This lesson sounds as if it was too ambitious either for you or for the class at this point in your career. Review what went wrong very carefully: too much going on at one time? Content not right for the class? No monitoring? Too many resources? You might want to review this with your mentor or teacher. Plan the next lesson to avoid the same mistakes. You could help yourself by asking the teacher to work with you in a TA role in your next lesson. Everyone has some poor lessons but you will learn from these as well as from the good ones.

5. **'My mentor has asked me to teach some non-core subject lessons but my friend who is doing the same training in a different school has not been asked to do this. I think I would rather stick with the core subjects at the moment. Can I do this?'**

Check your course expectations for this part of your school based training. Unless it specifies you will teach only core subjects you cannot do this. Your mentor may have identified teaching other subjects as your current training need. Your training needs will probably be different from your friend's because you and your school are different. I suggest you check your course documentation, discuss it with your mentor and see teaching a wide range of subjects as a step onward in your professional development.

Setting homework

Setting homework is an important task for you as it allows you to address Teachers' Standard, Part One, 4 which includes the ability to 'set homework and plan other out-of-class activities to consolidate and extend the knowledge and understanding pupils have acquired' (p. 13). Homework is not statutory in schools in England and, indeed, its educational value is dubious in terms of the difference it makes to pupils' academic outcomes.

However, it is a very important way of engaging parents in their children's education. It is also valuable in giving parents the opportunity to demonstrate solidarity and support for the school by encouraging and supporting the completion of homework. Homework may also help children to develop their independence, self-organisation and responsibility.

To see how much homework children should have in your school, you need to look at the school policy. The official recommendations (proposed in 1998) suggested that even at the end of Key Stage 2 children should not have more than 30 minutes of homework a day. This homework might consist of:

- **taking books (or story sacks) home to read with parents or a sibling, a practice that has demonstrated benefits even where parents do not speak English;**
- **taking home mathematics games to play with family members;**
- **homework sheets containing simple, planned work that does not demand elaborate resources and that can be done with parents or siblings;**
- **asking children to research a particular topic;**
- **asking children to ask family members questions about a particular topic;**
- **regular learning of spellings or multiplication tables for tests.**

All these count as homework and an Early Years trainee is likely to set homework in the form of books or story sacks; as a Primary trainee you may set spellings and worksheets. You might set homework on paper or use the school's network or website. This choice depends on what the rest of the school does and on the expectations of parents.

Make sure you know the school routine for setting homework.

- **When do children take it home?**
- **When does it come back?**
- **Is there any marking to be done? If so, what sort of response is required?**
- **Find out how schools establish expectations in their parents. Most schools will have hand outs for parents about topics like using story sacks, reading with your child, learning spellings, accessing homework on the network, etc. Many schools will organise parent workshops to introduce these ideas to parents.**

When setting homework make sure you:

- **give children a reasonable time to complete the work (they may not be able to do all it on the same day) but not so long that they forget it;**
- **explain homework clearly and ensure that any sheets are sent home with brief instructions for parents;**
- **ensure that homework does not need much in the way of resources, as parents may not be able to find them at short notice;**
- **establish a routine that children and parents will remember easily;**
- **set work that everyone has equal access to – you cannot expect parents to drop everything and rush off to the library;**
- **praise children for doing homework – however poor the results, the child has made an effort and shown commitment;**
- **have consistent, non-judgemental expectations of all children – if you have set the homework appropriately you should expect all children to achieve it, whatever their social situation;**
- **support children who repeatedly fail to do homework by discussing it carefully, ensuring they understand and, if all else fails, giving them time to do it in school.**

Setting, managing and marking homework is a very small part of your training but it is something you can easily achieve and feel satisfied about.

Professional values and the wider life of the school

As part of addressing the Teachers' Standards you will need to demonstrate that you can fulfil wider professional responsibilities, including:

- **make a positive contribution to the wider life and ethos of the school**
- **develop effective professional relationships with colleagues, knowing how and when to draw on advice and specialist support**
- **deploy support staff effectively (Teachers' Standard, Part One, 8).**

Some features of school life are discussed in the early chapters of this book – punctuality, attendance at staff meetings and careful preparation. These demonstrate your commitment to your role as a teacher and mentors invariably mention these issues when writing reports about trainees' progress. However, you will have other opportunities to participate in the life of the school. Some of these will be low key, such as greeting parents at the beginning and end of the day and planning interesting displays of work. Others will be very high profile, such as being invited to go with the school on a residential trip to a study centre. Between these two extremes are all the events, routines and celebrations that are part of school life – sports day, Eid, Christmas, book week, the summer play, class assemblies, school clubs, the cross country or football team and day trips. Although they may seem a demanding extra dimension on top of daily planning and teaching, these are the events that allow us to share our values and enthusiasms with children. These events are every bit as educative as the formal curriculum and will also promote key skills such as cooperation and flexibility.

You will need to seek out some opportunities. For instance, if you want to know about the work of the governors in the school, you will need to do a little research on the internet and then arrange a meeting with a school governor, through your mentor. If you are well prepared, you can find out all you need to know in this way.

Trainees often worry about whether they have done enough to address The Standards relating to working with parents. You need to ensure you take opportunities to:

- **observe your teacher (and others) interacting with parents on a daily basis at the beginning and end of school;**
- **greet parents yourself (when this is appropriate);**
- **observe at a parents' evening or open day;**
- **discuss with a teacher the school's efforts to involve parents;**
- **ask to look at the literature that goes home from school to parents, including advice about reading with children, spelling sheets and school newsletters or bulletins.**

PRACTICAL TASK PRACTICAL TASK **PRACTICAL TASK** PRACTICAL TASK **PRACTICAL TASK**

Identify your opportunities to take a full professional role. Use the checklist below to identify what experiences you have already had (column 1) then use column 2 to identify some experiences to aim for in your next placement.

Table 5.2

Opportunity	Experienced	Identified for next placement
In the classroom		
Attendance register		
Welcome parents and carers before and after school		
Deal with absence notes		
Manage the collection and marking of homework (books to read, etc.)		
Set homework		
Create a display in your class		
Create an interactive area in the setting		
Other		
Beyond the classroom		
Set out and use the gym or hall		
Teach in the computer suite		
Teach on the field or playground		
Go on playground duty		
Attend a staff meeting		
Attend planning meetings		
Attend a whole staff Inset session		
Participate in a parents' evening		
Attend a PTA event		
Participate in a school visit		
Attend a governors' meeting or discuss it with a governor		
Play a musical instrument in assembly		
Run or participate in a class assembly		
Participate in an after school club or coaching		
Take part in a school visit		
Attend sports day		
Participate in a transition visit to a Key Stage 2 or 3 school		
Participate in a book, arts or charity day		
Attend the breakfast club		
Other		

Identify your opportunities to use a wide range of resources. Use the checklist below to identify what resources you have already used (column 1) then use column 2 to identify some resources you aim to use in your next placement.

(Continued)

(Continued)

Table 5.3

Resources selected and used	Last placement	Next placement
Write on a flipchart or whiteboard		
Selected story or poetry		
Use a visualizer		
Use a data projector		
Use an interactive whiteboard		
Use a video		
Use a radio programme		
Use a digital recorder		
Use reprographic equipment		
Teach using a set of laptops/tablets		
Use IT for preparation and planning		
Set out and use the gym or hall		
Use the outdoor classroom or field		
Other		

School visits

Ideally, during the time you are in the school, you will have the opportunity to plan a visit to another setting. This might be a visit to a museum, gallery, supermarket, DIY store or local park. To plan for this, work through the following checklist with your teacher.

Checklist for out-of-school visits

Do you have information about?

Table 5.4

School's policy on trips to include: • Adult/pupil ratio/supervision • Charging for school trips • Using transport for school trips • First aid/inhalers • Insurance in relation to school trips • Emergency procedures • Exploratory visit by trip leader	
Risk assessment procedures	
Information to pupils	
DfES guidance on health and safety of pupils on educational visits	

LA/TSA/ Academy guidance on health and safety of pupils on educational visits	
Letter/consent form proformas	
Proposal form for HT outlining the objectives, cost, intended leaving/returning times and cost estimate	
Schedule of trips planned for the year across the whole school	
School's procedures on parents' information evenings/sessions in relation to school trips	
Other guidance used in school	
Useful contacts used by the school	
Specific details of a trip already undertaken or to be taken in the current school year	

Communication with parents and carers

As a trainee you will need to 'communicate effectively with parents with regard to pupils' achievements and well-being' (Teachers' Standards, Part One, 8), but you will do this under the supervision of your teacher and only in a limited way. This does not stop you from learning about the processes of communication in your setting. These might include any of the following:

- **school newsletters and blogs;**
- **school-run reading or mathematics schemes;**
- **parent-run projects like story sack workshops;**
- **the daily communication of meeting parents delivering and collecting their children;**
- **home visits for those children starting in a new setting;**
- **parents coming into school to do a regular activity like cooking with children;**
- **parents or grandparents coming in to talk to pupils about a topic;**
- **routine parents' evenings or day workshops;**
- **written reports to parents.**

Some of these opportunities are more readily available to you in certain placements. For instance, if you are placed in the Early Years Foundation Stage you are almost certain to have the chance to meet parents or carers and talk to them at the beginning and end of the session. If you are in Key Stage 2, you may only see parents at formal parents' evenings. If you are fortunate enough to be in school for parents' evenings or home visits you should ask to sit in. You will not usually have a real role in reporting but you will be able to observe the teacher at work. Writing reports for parents is a task you should undertake at some time during your school based training. Collect evidence of the attainment of a few children and write mock reports, using the school system.

Completing school-based tasks

As part of your training you will almost certainly have a range of tasks that are an important part of your learning experience. These may be tasks arranged by your mentor to ensure you have appropriate learning experiences. They may be tasks connected to assignments or dissertations or they may be tasks set by your course tutors to contribute to your development and, possibly, your taught sessions. It would be easy to see these tasks as a distraction from the business of teaching, but they do help to ensure you have the necessary range of experiences to meet The Standards or to complete academic parts of your qualification. Never ignore these tasks nor leave planning them until the placement is well underway. Plan these tasks right at the beginning of the placement so that you can see what you have to do week by week, then build them into your timetable for the week. If you are undertaking school-based tasks or a research project in school, there are some key points to think about at the start of the time in the class.

- **Ensure you are totally clear about what school-based tasks or projects you need to accomplish during the time you are doing school based training. Although other tasks may well be suggested as part of your training, those you start out with are essential. If you don't plan for them you won't accomplish them.**
- **Review the aims and scope of your tasks or project and ensure you can achieve them in the time available. Make sure, if you are addressing a particular research question, that you are clear how you will collect evidence. If you have school-based tasks, be clear about how much written evidence you need.**
- **Look at your course documentation or talk with your mentor to establish what proportion of time you should spend on your tasks or study. You can then negotiate appropriate times around your teaching commitments.**
- **Check that you are able to work with the resources or pupils you need. Sometimes school plans change suddenly and you may need to re-negotiate.**
- **Where there is background reading or research to do to prepare for your tasks or study, ensure you have done as much as possible before the teaching starts. In this way your tasks will be well focused and you will waste less of your precious time.**
- **Check that any research you want to carry out with children or teachers in your school is ethical and professionally appropriate. If you are part of a course based in a university or college, the institution will have guidelines on this.**
- **Review your project or tasks and list the school staff you would like to talk to or observe. If you are ready with this list, you can discuss it with your mentor.**

Some tasks will be routine teaching that you would do anyway, others may encourage you to focus on a particular aspect of the curriculum or a group of children. Consider each task carefully and be clear about what you will need to do to accomplish it.

For example, a task may require an in-depth look at a small group of pupils. Now is the time to ask yourself some questions.

- **Have you identified this group?**
- **Are these pupils from your own class or will you need to identify pupils from another class or age group?**
- **Have you spoken to your mentor about arranging a visit to another class and to the teacher concerned?**
- **Do you know where the individual pupils fit into the academic range of the class?**
- **How much time is needed in order to carry out these tasks?**
- **Have you discussed them with your class teacher and school mentor?**
- **Have you planned time in which you can carry out these tasks?**
- **Once you have carried out the tasks, will you need to set aside time to complete any writing up?**
- **Consider whether you should share this information with anyone and how you will ensure it is confidential.**

Discuss your school-based tasks with your mentor early on in your placement and monitor them at mentor meetings. This is a very good opportunity for you to demonstrate a professional, organised approach to your work. If you are planning and working through school-based tasks you appear very much more organised and competent than if you leave them until the last fortnight and then panic.

If you are doing a project or study involving the children or teachers in your school you will have to make decisions about how far you share data you collect with the children or teachers. Whatever you decide, you should ensure that you have the full consent of all participants in any study and that you anonymise the names of pupils, teachers and schools in such a way that they cannot be identified in any report or dissertation.

REFLECTIVE TASK

Audit the range of:

- **pupil groupings;**
- **resources;**
- **interactive learning strategies (questions, etc.) you have used on placement so far.**

Complete the chart with your examples.

Table 5.5

Learning objective	Pupil grouping	Resources (including e-resources)	Interactive teaching/ learning strategies
	Whole class or group		Small whiteboards
	Individual pupil	Self-selected book	
	Ability group		
	Mixed ability group		

Which opportunities have you missed so far? When can you plan to try out a grouping or teaching strategy you have not used so far?

A SUMMARY OF KEY POINTS

- Being well prepared and appearing confident are key factors in successful teaching.
- You should ask a range of question types and ensure you question a whole range of children. Questioning is a skilled business and you can practise and improve your questioning so that it is a useful differentiation tool.

(Continued)

(Continued)

- Interactive teaching means involving children actively in their learning. It can increase learning in whole-class and group settings. School based training is your chance to develop your use of interactive teaching.

- Homework is a term covering a wide range of activities. Get involved with whatever counts as homework and be thoughtful in setting work for children.

- School based training offers a wider range of opportunities for you to demonstrate your values and become involved in the school – seize these opportunities.

- Successful completion of school-based tasks depends on planning for their completion early in your placement.

RESOURCES RESOURCES **RESOURCES** RESOURCES RESOURCES **RESOURCES**

Some information and discussion about the role and responsibilities of teachers can be found at http://teachwellnow.blogspot.co.uk/2012/03/classroom-teacher-roles-and.html

Information for school governors (including roles and responsibilities) can be found at: http://www.nga.org.uk/Be-a-Governor.aspx. Look at this site before you meet your governors.

Official guidelines on planning learning experiences out of school can be found in the DfE publication 'Health and safety: advice on legal duties and powers', to be found at https://www.gov.uk/government/uploads/system/uploads/attachment_data/file/335111/DfE_Health_and_Safety_Advice_06_02_14.pdf

6
Learning to assess, monitor and report on children's progress

Learning outcomes

By the end of this chapter you should:

- **know the main types of assessment;**
- **know what assessment tasks you need to engage in;**
- **know the role of target-setting.**

Assessing and monitoring

This chapter summarises some key points about assessment. You need to demonstrate that you can 'make accurate and productive use of assessment' (Teachers' Standards, Part One, 6). You need to:

- **know and understand how to assess the relevant subject and curriculum areas, including statutory assessment requirements;**
- **make use of formative and summative assessment to secure pupils' progress;**
- **use relevant data to monitor progress, set targets, and plan subsequent lessons;**
- **give pupils regular feedback, both orally and through accurate marking, and encourage pupils to respond to the feedback.**

You should know what the children can do, note what they have done and identify what they and you need to do next. It is also important to be able to share this information with parents, children and at a school and government level to measure individual, school and national progress. This is the role of assessment. The two main types of assessment you will encounter are formative and summative.

Formative assessment (assessment for learning, or AfL) is assessment that directly contributes to your teaching. Each time you teach a lesson you assess what the children have achieved relative to your objective. You then act on this by planning the next lesson to take account of how well the children achieved your objective. In the Early Years Foundation Stage, a great deal of observation is planned to assess how children are developing in all areas of the curriculum. This is supplemented by work done by children and records of discussions with children. In all the Key Stages, your formative assessment (or assessment for learning) is principally conducted to inform your teaching but any records you keep may also be used as a basis for teacher assessments which are summative.

Summative assessment (assessment of learning, or AoL) is assessment that gives you a snapshot of the child's achievement at a particular time. It is particularly useful assessment for reporting to parents or to government. The most obvious examples are the

Statutory National Tests and teacher assessments carried out towards the end of Key Stage 1 and 2 and, from 2016, in Reception. The results of these are reported to government, children and parents in order to monitor school performance, and gauge individual progress. This information is also used by government and schools to make judgements about school success, and set targets. In EYFS the Foundation Stage Profile may still be used to collect evidence from formative assessments and report a summative judgement about a child's progress to the parents and school at the start of Key Stage 1, although it ceases to be statutory in 2016, and may not be used in every setting.

Assessment is theoretically very simple but can be difficult to organise and manage in practice. Assessment aims to establish what children know, understand and can do. There are only three sources of evidence you can assess: what the children know, what they do and what they produce. The simplest ways to assess these things are to:

- **ask children what they know and note what they say;**
- **observe what they do and make notes (or take photos);**
- **collect and annotate what they produce in their schoolwork and tests.**

These are your sources of evidence. In practice it is rather trickier than this because teachers are trying to make balanced assessments of a huge range of skills, knowledge and understanding for all the children in the class. Moreover, you are aiming to keep a record of your assessments, but do so in such a way that still allows time for teaching. Managing this will always be a challenge.

In school based training there are a number of key assessment and recording experiences you should seek to have, although you might not have all of these early in your school based training.

Giving feedback and making assessments

Giving feedback and making assessments as you teach is vital. ('Use relevant data to monitor progress, set targets, and plan subsequent lessons.' Teachers' Standards, Part One, 6.) This sort of assessment should be part of your teaching from the outset. You need to be clear when giving feedback. Do not praise wrong answers. Indicate that they are wrong but do not dwell on them. Where an answer to a question is partially correct, emphasise the correct part. Where a child has an obvious misconception, you need to explore this and find out why. Praise children often, but not so effusively that praise becomes routine and meaningless. Make sure the child knows why you are praising them.

The same is true of marking. Poor marking may simply pick out every error, give no ideas for improvement and demoralise the pupils or simply be so uninformative (a tick, for instance) that it means virtually nothing except that you have seen the work. Good marking acknowledges the child's achievements but identifies where they could improve and how to do it. You must read your school marking policy and ask your teacher to check you are using it effectively. Once you can do this, the children's work becomes valuable evidence for your use in meeting the Teachers' Standards.

Recording attainment on your lesson plans

Recording pupil achievement on your lesson plan is a basic type of assessment you can start right from the beginning of the placement. The key to this is identifying clear statements of what you are looking for in your lesson plans that will allow you to assess who achieved the objectives of the session (or lesson).

For example, in one particular lesson you may find that a large number of children found the objective too challenging. In response, you have to amend your next lesson to revisit some aspects of the earlier content. Alternatively, you may find that the objective was not challenging enough for some children and realise you have to provide more challenge for them in the next lesson. This is good teaching and a canny trainee will make quite sure that mentors can see that you do change your lesson plans in response to the outcomes of previous lessons. Some trainees deliberately highlight changes to lesson plans to emphasise that their responses to assessment are to do something in their teaching.

Recording the attainment of the whole group

Recording the attainment of the whole group, so that someone else can see your record and understand it, is the next step. To do this you can use a class or group grid, which will give you a very easy recording format but little detail. You can use a system of ticks or stars to show how well the objective has been addressed. This format should be adapted as appropriate, with columns and headings to suit circumstances. Records should be dated, systematic, regularly updated, manageable and should clearly summarise learning and inform future teaching. Names of pupils may be arranged to reflect class groupings and should be confidential.

Comments on significant individual responses may also be evident in lesson/activity plan assessments and evaluations with points considered for the next lesson/activity.

Table 6.1 A simple chart to record pupil attainment

Class/Group	Subject/Area of Learning..............................
Names of Pupils	Experience and Achievement

Compiling a pupil profile

A pupil profile will give you an overview of an individual child and also show you just how much varied evidence you need to make judgements about performance. You may well be asked to do this for a number of pupils as a directed task on placement.

Pupil profile (Key Stage 1 or 2)
This record is designed to reflect pupil progress during the placement:

- **to contribute to the school's own pupil records;**
- **to provide evidence to support reporting to parents.**

This record may be adapted to suit the balance of areas taught.

Table 6.2 A sample format for a pupil profile (Key Stage 1 or 2)

Name of pupil .... Class ....

Subject	Comments (dated entries to record key points in learning)
English	
Mathematics	
Science	
Art and Design	
Computing	
Design and Technology	
Languages (KS2 only)	
Geography	
History	
Music	
Physical Education	
Religious Education	

Key targets for pupil's development:

- **completed by end of school experience;**
- **based on evidence in the profile above.**

Pupil profile (Early Years Foundation Stage)

This record is designed to reflect pupil progress during the placement:

- **to contribute to the school's own pupil records or Early Years Foundation Stage Profile;**
- **to provide evidence to support reporting to parents.**

This record may be adapted to suit the balance of areas taught.

Table 6.3 A sample format for a pupil profile (Early Years Foundation Stage)

Name of pupil .... Class ....

Area of learning		Comments (dated entries to record progress in learning)
Prime	communication and language	
Prime	physical development	
Prime	personal, social and emotional development	
Specific	Literacy	
Specific	Mathematics	
Specific	understanding the world	
Specific	expressive arts and design	

Key targets for pupil's development:

- **completed at end of school experience;**
- **based on evidence in profile.**

National assessment requirements

Although the National Curriculum is only statutory in maintained schools, assessing children's work against the criteria at the end of a key stage (statements of attainment) is statutory for all state funded schools, including academies and free schools. Independent schools may choose to do it. Summative assessment at the end of years other than Year 2 and Year 6 is not statutory, so schools set their own expected levels of performance. This means that you need to know about end of KS assessment, wherever you are training. This is why Teachers' Standards, Part One, 6 demands you 'know and understand how to assess the relevant subject and curriculum areas, including statutory assessment requirements'.

The system is currently in transition from the old curriculum and its assessments to the new 2014 curriculum. Pupils working in Y2 and 6 in 2014–15 used the old curriculum, which had separate statements of attainment, but will transfer to the new curriculum in 2015–16, like all other children. Assessment for the children working on the old curriculum, included 'levelling' against the old 'attainment targets' at age related levels. In 2015 the last Y2 and Y6 classes assessed against the old curriculum will use SATs and levels. The goal for 2015 Y2 children is a level 2a and for Y6, level 4.

The new statutory national assessments for the 2014 curriculum will occur at key points in children's primary education. They aim to give a picture of school performance and to provide standard information to parents. The statutory assessments set out below complement on-going teacher assessment. From 2015–16, statutory assessment includes:

- **a statutory two-year-old progress check undertaken in Early Years settings which is already used and well embedded;**
- **a short Reception baseline that will sit within the assessments that teachers make of children during Reception. This will be used as the baseline when measuring school performance;**
- **a phonics check test near the end of Year 1, which is already established and used;**
- **a teacher assessment at the end of Key Stage 1 in mathematics; reading; and writing, informed by pupils' scores in externally set but internally marked tests (writing will be partly informed by the grammar, punctuation and spelling test); and teacher assessment of speaking and listening and science;**
- **externally set and externally marked national tests at the end of Key Stage 2 in: mathematics; reading; grammar, punctuation and spelling; and a teacher assessment of mathematics, reading, writing, and science.**

You should discuss all these with your school assessment co-ordinator and class teacher.

Key Stage 1

At the end of Key Stage 1, from 2016, teacher assessment in mathematics and reading will be informed by externally set, internally marked tests. There will also be an externally set test in grammar, punctuation and spelling which will help to inform the teacher assessment of writing. There are examples of these tests on the gov.uk website https://www.gov.uk/government/collections/national-curriculum-assessments-2016-sample-materials

The test results will be expressed as a scaled score, which means a score which has been translated from a raw score onto a score on a fixed, defined scale on which 100 is the target score for all children. This allows performance to be reported on a consistent scale for all children, which retains the same meaning from one year to the next. Therefore, a particular scaled score reflects the same level of attainment in one year as in the previous year, having adjusted for any differences in difficulty of the specific tests. Teacher assessment of speaking and listening, writing and science will continue. It is going to be very important to understand the performance descriptors.

The performance descriptors will inform statutory teacher assessments at the end of Key Stage 1 and results will be expressed in terms of these performance descriptors. For mathematics, reading, writing and speaking and listening, teachers will assess pupils as meeting one of several performance descriptors. For science, there will be a single performance descriptor of the new expected standard. These will be linked to the content of the new curriculum and drafts are currently available at https://www.gov.uk/government/uploads/system/uploads/attachment_data/file/368298/KS1-KS2_Performance_descriptors_consultation.pdf. Parents will be told which descriptor describes their child's performance.

Moderation of teacher assessments is very important and there will be moderation exercises within school and across schools to ensure, each year, that teachers have a shared understanding of the performance descriptors. You should try to arrange to attend this moderation or, at least, to discuss it with your mentor.

Key Stage 2

At the end of Key Stage 2 pupils will continue to sit externally set and marked tests in mathematics, reading, and grammar, punctuation and spelling. These will be used for school performance measures from 2016 onwards. As now, there will continue to be teacher assessment in mathematics, reading, writing and science to give a broader picture of children's attainment. As in Key Stage 1, the tests and assessments will reflect the content of the new curriculum.

New performance descriptors will inform the statutory teacher assessments at the end of Key Stage 2, and they are also available on gov.uk. For writing, teachers will assess pupils as meeting one of several performance descriptors. For science, reading and mathematics, there will be a single performance descriptor of the new expected standard. A sample of pupils will continue to sit tests in science to give a picture of national performance, usually every other year. As in KS1 you should aim to attend or understand the moderation of teacher assessment as well as the test process, which you can observe.

The results of the tests in reading; mathematics; and grammar, punctuation and spelling will be reported to pupils and parents as scaled scores. Parents will be provided with their child's score alongside the average for their school, the local area and nationally. To reach the new expected standard, each pupil will be required to attain a scaled score of 100 or more in the tests in reading and mathematics, as well as being assessed by their teacher as reaching the new expected standard in writing.

If children reach 'mastery standard' in the assessments in 2016 or beyond, they will not go on to the next key stage, but explore their key stage in more depth. This is a major change in approach from previous assessment practices and offers children opportunities for interesting, in-depth work.

One very important aspect of the new assessment mechanisms at Foundation KS, KS1 and KS2 is that it is designed to hold schools accountable for pupil outcomes and these will be used to judge school effectiveness. The new 'floor standard' will be 85 per cent of pupils reaching the expected standard in each area of the curriculum assessed statutorily at the end of KS2. A school will be given an 'attainment standard' based on the proportion of pupils reaching the new expected standard in all of reading, writing and mathematics. A school will be above the attainment floor if 85 per cent of pupils reach the new expected standard in each area. This means that your school will have a process for setting targets for each class to ensure the school meets the floor standard. You must discuss these with your teacher and try to attend any staff meetings about these targets.

Observing the administration of Statutory National Tests

Observation will be important whatever age phase you are training to teach. These tests are used to provide a summative (or snapshot) assessment of children's achievements at the end of a key stage (or at the end of Year 1 in the case of the Phonics Skills Check). The actual tests are, of course, secret until just before they are used, but sample tests and marking schemes have been published online and the new framework of testing will be fully in place in the summer of 2016. From 2015, the National Tests for English and maths will be marked, externally, on screen. The best way to keep up to date with the kinds of statutory tests that primary schools are required to use is to consult the Department for Education National Curriculum website at https://www.gov.uk/government/collections/national-curriculum#curriculum-assessment.

If you are an Early Years trainee you should observe the Reception Baseline assessment, the Phonics Skills Check and other Key Stage 1 National Tests during the summer term of your school based training. If you are a Primary trainee you should observe both the Key Stage 1 and Key Stage 2 National Tests. Statutory National Tests may not be taking place in your class. You should talk with your mentor and arrange to visit the classes where the tasks and tests are happening.

It is not enough to observe how the tests are administered. Test preparation is very important to both children and teachers. We know that 'testwiseness' (that is familiarity with the format and expectations of a test) is very important and may make a huge difference to scores. Therefore, all teachers prepare their children with practice items and, as everyone does this, not to do it would disadvantage your children. You must ask your teacher and mentor about this. You must also understand how they are marked and how those marks are used. Whichever tests you observe, please take the time to look through a test handbook so that you know what you are seeing and how the marks are arrived at.

MINI CASE MINI CASE **MINI CASE** **MINI CASE** MINI CASE **MINI CASE** **MINI CASE**

Assessment has been a bit of a roller coaster for me. In my first term I worked on assessing English and maths and though it took a long time, I could understand how the tracking worked. Then in term 2, I helped on the Phonics screening in Y1 and, when I understood it, that really built my confidence. It all came together in Term 3, when I observed the national tests at both key stages and really talked through how the results informed targets. I think the training session run by University in Term 2 helped because I could see how the teacher tracking and tests came together. The class targets are really daunting, though. Those targets made me realise assessment is really strategic and not just a paper exercise.

Manish

Contributing to the EYFS Profile or school reports

This is a very important aspect of assessment. You need to collect a wide range of evidence and ensure that your comments highlight what the child has achieved and what is now the target. In 2015, the Early Years Foundation Stage Profile will still exist and you should write some mock entries if you are an Early Years trainee. If you are unsure of the format of the EYFS Profile, there is some very clear guidance on the DfE website at https://www.gov.uk/government/publications/early-years-foundation-stage-profile-handbook.

Whether you are training to teach EY or Primary, you should write some mock Profiles or reports (perhaps using the school report software) and scrutinise these with your teacher or mentor.

Some useful guidelines for writing reports for parents about children's progress are summarised below:

- **Reports should be written for parents in a clear and straightforward way, avoiding unnecessary National Curriculum jargon bearing in mind that pupils often read their reports, and parents are usually most interested in the overview.**
- **Comments should be kept brief and clear.**
- **Reports need to refer to whether or not the pupil is happy, settled, and behaving well.**
- **There should be advice to parents about how they can help and support their child.**
- **There should be reference to attainment and progress within the subject areas, but this can be general enough to suggest breadth and specific enough to give parents clear understanding of progress.**
- **The report should also include reference to national expectations for children of a similar age.**
- **Effort as well as attainment should be recognised.**
- **There should be reference to strengths and areas for improvement with some targets for improvement clearly identified, particularly for core subjects. (There is no requirement to include a target for every subject.)**
- **Attendance and percentages of unauthorised absences should be included, and in addition, there may be reference to punctuality.**
- **Report formats will vary according to the age/stage of the pupils and can be customised appropriately.**
- **In all cases, parents should be provided with an opportunity for discussing their child's report.**

Setting targets for children

During school experience you will also be expected to use your records of assessment to set realistic and demanding targets for your pupils.

You also need to be aware of government targets, e.g. in areas such as English and mathematics, as well as school targets based on a variety of data including schools' test scores in relationship to those of similar schools – benchmarking.

It is now a legal requirement for schools to set improvement targets in core curriculum areas, and they are encouraged to do so in other aspects of school life. You will find that teachers in schools have been setting targets for several years, so you will become aware of the processes they employ when seeking school and pupil improvement.

Setting targets in the classroom

When setting targets in the classroom, you should consider:

- **school targets (obtain a copy of the relevant information);**
- **issues affecting the whole class (academic and non-academic);**
- **issues affecting groups within the class (academic and non-academic);**
- **issues affecting individuals within the class (academic and non-academic).**

Consult your class teacher or mentor about these.

Setting targets for classroom improvement

When setting targets with pupils, the process already established for your own target-setting may be used, with minor changes. You will need to start with pupils' current knowledge, understanding, skills, behaviour patterns, etc. – review. However, in place of the Teachers' Standards, you will need to consider targets and policies already in place within your school, key stage or classroom – school targets. The rest of the process follows the same route as your own target-setting.

The nature of target-setting with pupils varies. Some targets will be long term and may feature school priorities that are in the challenging zone. You will almost certainly need to work through the planning cycle (Figure 6.1), record your plan and share it with all those involved. On other occasions, for example after marking pupils' work, it might be sufficient to agree a target in the comfort zone with the pupils and write it on the board or in the pupils' books.

As you get used to the target-setting process, you will be able to use the key headings as a checklist and begin to write down only what is necessary. Whenever possible, try to involve pupils in setting targets so that eventually they will be able to use the process for themselves.

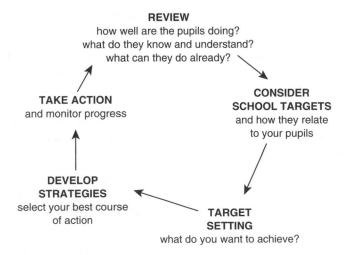

REVIEW
how well are the pupils doing?
what do they know and understand?
what can they do already?

CONSIDER SCHOOL TARGETS
and how they relate
to your pupils

TAKE ACTION
and monitor progress

TARGET SETTING
what do you want to achieve?

DEVELOP STRATEGIES
select your best course
of action

Figure 6.1 Target-setting as part of a cycle for improvement

Working with elements of the cycle

Reviewing

Before you set targets with your pupils you need to review with them their current performance in the area designated for improvement. Evidence relating to how well pupils are doing may be obtained from a variety of sources and used when setting individual, group or whole-class targets. You might consider, where appropriate:

- **pupils' exercise books, pictures or work folders;**
- **records of assessments made by you, your teacher and other practitioners;**
- **displays of pupils' work;**
- **comments made by the class teacher or other colleagues, including annotations on saved work giving the context and task;**
- **your own observations within and outside the classroom;**
- **the pupils' comments related to the proposed area for development.**

When reviewing you should:

- **use appropriate evidence of pupils' current performance;**
- **discuss the current situation with pupils and obtain their perspective. You could get them to carry out a simple self-evaluation.**

Working with school targets

Schools will have established their own targets and you will need to find out what these are and feature them in target-setting with your pupils. There will be some targets that reflect national priorities such as English and mathematics. These will have been set when schools analysed the data from their annual tests. The national data, known as the School Performance Tables, are produced jointly by the DfE and Ofsted and are available in December of each year (http://www.education.gov.uk/schools/performance/). They contain national summary results, value added information and benchmark information. The data are also available to individual schools through the RAISEonline system (https://www.raiseonline.org). There are some main areas of analysis possible through these systems:

- **school level analyses comparing the school results in the key stage tests and teacher assessments with schools similar to them (in terms of either eligibility for free school meals or prior attainment);**
- **pupil value added – comparing the progress of individual pupils or groups of pupils between key stages with progress nationally;**
- **question analysis allowing schools to see how their pupils performed in each of the questions in the National Curriculum tests compared to performance nationally – so that teaching can address those test questions where pupils have performed poorly.**

The system also helps the school to set targets for individual pupils in the light of projections based on progress by similar pupils in the best performing schools with a similar baseline. You should try to discuss this with the responsible person in your school.

Each teacher will be expected to contribute to the achievement of these targets. This will mean setting targets at the appropriate level for the pupils in the class. Where targets are long term, it will be necessary to break them down into manageable steps.

You may not know the full details of school targets but you should aim to find out what those targets are and how they affect your class.

When working with school targets you should:

- find out what the school's targets are and how they relate to the school's performance data;
- discuss with your class teacher what the appropriate targets for the pupils in your class are and how these are being addressed;
- ensure that targets you set with pupils support, rather than conflict with, school targets and aims.

Target-setting

You will be asked to identify, with the pupils, clear and measurable targets that take them forward from their current performance. When schools set targets they are encouraged to think SMART: specific, measurable, achievable, realistic, time related.

They are also asked to set challenging targets in areas of high priority – targets in the challenging zone; as well as those where success is readily achievable – targets in the comfort zone. You may set targets for the whole class, a group or individuals. The targets may be in academic or non-academic areas and be short or long term.

When setting targets you should:

- consider your review of pupils' work and pupil self-evaluation;
- consider school targets, class targets, etc.;
- write lesson/session/day targets (or learning objectives) clearly on the board;
- make long-/medium-term class targets (e.g. rules) clearly visible and refer to them;
- make individuals' targets clearly visible, e.g. use a particular colour when you or they write targets in their books (some non-academic targets can be written on small cards and taped to the pupils' tables);
- communicate with parents on a daily basis, sharing the targets with the home and let parents know of successful achievements;
- make your targets:

  o SMART;
  o in the challenging as well as the comfort zone.

- make certain that the pupils have a clear picture in their minds of what success will look like. Get them to tell you what they understand to be a successful outcome. Check that it matches your criteria.

Developing strategies

You now need to think of ways to put your carefully framed targets into action. When developing strategies to improve pupils' performance, you may consult with mentors, tutors and other students, read appropriate articles and books, or brainstorm. However, when working with pupils you will mainly be discussing their targets with them. If possible let them make suggestions and thus acquire some ownership of the strategies about to be implemented. You must be careful to avoid dashing into action with your first idea without considering its implications or alternatives that might be more promising.

When developing strategies you should:

- consider a number of possible courses of action and include pupils in discussing them;
- select actions most likely to succeed;
- consider what support you will need to implement the plan;
- list any resources you will require to implement the plan;
- when necessary, have a timetable for implementing the various parts of the plan.

Taking action and monitoring progress

While implementing your strategies, you will need to check that you are on track by reviewing and monitoring progress made by the pupils. You may wish to enlist the help of the pupils in keeping records of their progress. In doing this you can be creative in designing, or encouraging pupils to design, appropriate recording sheets. You will find that some pupils will be used to discussing their progress and will be developing their understanding and language about this whilst others will have less experience and find it hard to monitor and discuss their progress. Even the youngest child in the Early Years Foundation Stage can begin to plan, do and review what has been done and that reflection can be learned early on.

When monitoring progress you should:

- **consider with the pupils their progress against the targets, using records as evidence;**
- **consider with the pupils progress in relation to the time scales;**
- **decide if you need to reconsider your strategies with the pupils;**
- **decide with the pupils if you need to modify the targets.**

Actively involving children

When working with children you should try to increase motivation by giving them some ownership of the target-setting, monitoring and recording processes. Celebrate children's success. How does the school do this – awards, certificates, stickers, displays, etc.? Discuss this with teachers, mentors and children. You can set and celebrate targets in many aspects of school life. Be creative.

Always be aware of the importance of recognising success when pupils achieve their targets. This reinforces desirable behaviour patterns, helps to develop self-esteem and encourages even greater effort. Children's achievements need to be recognised across the curriculum and opportunities for success must be provided. Work needs to be differentiated so that it is set at an appropriate level and there is also the element of challenge. This enables children to strive for and achieve success (see Figure 6.2).

appropriate and challenging work

↓

striving to reach attainable goals

↓

successful experience

↓

developing confidence and self esteem

↓

further motivation

Figure 6.2 Achieving success

REFLECTIVE TASK

Plan a discussion with the assessment co-ordinator in your school. Ask some of the following questions:

- **What are the school improvement targets?**
- **How were these targets identified?**
- **Who has been involved in addressing these targets?**

Then consider how the school targets are reflected in the curricular planning for your class.

A SUMMARY OF KEY POINTS

- Assessment and monitoring of pupil performance begins with clear planning. Ensure your assessment criteria are included in your plans and evaluate them.
- Assessment, planning, target-setting and teaching are processes in a cycle that generates learning and school improvement.
- Schools, classes and pupils will all be working with targets for improvement and you need to know what these are.
- You will need to discuss target-setting in school with your teacher or mentor at two levels – whole-school targets and how your class are addressing these; and targets for individuals and groups in the class.
- There are key assessment experiences you should have at some time in your placements. These include routine evaluations and record keeping, levelling of children's work in various curriculum areas, completion of pupil profiles, completion of school reports, contribution to the Early Years Foundation Stage Profile and observation of statutory tasks and tests.

RESOURCES RESOURCES **RESOURCES** RESOURCES RESOURCES **RESOURCES**

The RAISEonline (Reporting and Analysis for Improvement through school Self-Evaluation) web site is at: https://www.raiseonline.org/

The DfE School Performance tables are available at: http://www.education.gov.uk/schools/performance/

National Union of Teachers (2009) *NUT Briefing: Target-Setting*. www.teachers.org.uk/files/NUT-BRIEF-TARGET-SETTING0109_KDR.doc

Martinez, P. (2001) *Great expectations: setting targets for students*. London: Learning and Skills Development Agency. http://dera.ioe.ac.uk/11308/1/012040.pdf

Many local authorities and school alliances have produced their own guidelines on target-setting. Try to acquire a copy of that produced by the local authority closest to your school.

7

Individualised training: target-setting, observation and assessment in your school based training

Learning outcomes

The experience of school based training is different for every trainee. You have a unique background and experience and each class you encounter is different. In this section we examine key issues for you as a trainee – how your placement is shaped, directed, monitored and assessed. You need to understand these processes to use them purposefully.

By the end of this chapter you will:

- **know what to expect when you are observed;**
- **understand the role of target-setting in your professional development and how to set targets;**
- **know how to prepare for, conduct and follow up mentor meetings;**
- **be able to manage and prepare for your assessment against the Teachers' Standards;**
- **recognise the link between your placement and your professional development as an NQT.**

Observation

One of the most useful experiences you can expect to have as part of your training is to be observed teaching. It is also one of the most realistic professional experiences you will have because teachers are observed throughout their careers. You will see that teachers in your placement schools observe each other, are observed by subject co-ordinators, head teachers, local authority advisers and Ofsted inspectors.

During your initial teacher training you will be observed by a number of people:

- **your class teacher;**
- **your mentor;**
- **your course tutor;**
- **subject specialists or head teachers in the school;**
- **external and internal examiners;**
- **Ofsted inspectors.**

These observations, and the feedback and target-setting they give rise to, are your chance to address Teachers' Standards, Part One, 8 and show that you can respond to advice and feedback from colleagues.

Observation by your class teacher

Most day-to-day observation will be done in an informal way, simply because the teacher is in the classroom with you. Unless you ask otherwise, he or she may give you only a few words of feedback. This sort of observation is valuable as the teacher will build up a comprehensive picture of your performance across the whole range of subjects and in a variety of settings – the class, the hall, the outside classroom, etc. These observations, however informal, will inevitably contribute to your assessment because the mentor is likely to discuss them with the class teacher.

You can focus these observations so that they work for you. Ask your teacher to observe you in specific sessions where you are addressing one of your targets, whether it is to teach using the school tablets, to manage children positively in the outdoor classroom or to use a more varied range of questions. You will need to discuss your plan and give a copy of it to the teacher as part of the observation. When giving you feedback, your teacher will pick out what you did well and suggest things you can do to continue progress. He or she will certainly see that you are focusing on improvement and looking for advice and this, in itself, is good practice. It would be unrealistic to expect full, detailed feedback for every lesson or session you teach and you should not assume that a lack of comment from your teacher indicates something negative. If you would like your teacher's insights about some aspect of your teaching and you have not asked him or her to observe the session, make sure you ask specific questions. Questions like 'What did you think about the worksheet I used?' or 'Do you think the tasks were at the right level for blue group?' are much more likely to have useful answers than general questions like 'How did it go?'

MINI CASE MINI CASE **MINI CASE** MINI CASE **MINI CASE** MINI CASE **MINI CASE**

Actually teaching in front of my teacher on first placement was agony to start with. I just hadn't expected it, really. The worst bit was that I was desperate for feedback. No – for praise. I only wanted to hear good stuff. If my teacher didn't say 'That was good' I felt despondent and I hung around hopefully at the end of every lesson. After the first week I got used to it and could discuss lessons rationally and even accept tips for the future, which was her way of giving advice. In my second week my teacher gave a sort of wave and nipped out of one lesson. I think it was the first time I realised that she wasn't scrutinising my every movement. It also made me realise I was in charge – at least for a bit.

Harbahavan, PGCE trainee

In my first class I was totally relaxed about teaching in front of my class teacher because I'd worked in her class for a while. She offered reassuring comments whenever I taught. I wasn't really prepared for how different it would be when I went to another class on placement. Initially, I felt nervous teaching in front of someone else but I got used to it quickly. It was harder to get used to the way he often didn't comment about my teaching every time I taught a lesson. I found myself asking 'How was it?' all the time. As the placement went on, I realised that my teacher did comment, but just not about everything I taught, and I relaxed about it. I also found that he was really pleased to be asked to observe a lesson and talk through the good and bad points after – he just liked to be asked to do it. I think he really didn't want to be over-critical and make me feel I was being observed in every lesson. The placement went really well and I learned a lot from that teacher.

Maureen, SCITT Partnership Trainee

Observation by your mentor

Your mentor, or sometimes your class teacher, will do more formal observations. The number of these will vary but you can expect at least one formal, written observation a fortnight, including those of the course tutor and other staff, over the length of your school based training. You will agree times for these in advance and make sure a copy of your planning for the session or lesson is available to your mentor at the start of the observation. These observations will usually be recorded on a sheet (paper or electronic) with a specific format (although these vary from course to course) and comments will be linked to the standards and your targets. You will be given a copy of the feedback shortly after the observation and have a chance to discuss the observation with your mentor in your mentor meeting, if not before.

Some of these observations will be general, in the sense that they are observations of you teaching a particular subject, such as PSHE, or in a particular setting, such as the outdoor classroom. The mentor will pick out particular points, usually relevant to pupil learning, your planning, teaching and assessment in the lessons, and link these to the standards. As a result of each observation you will be clear about some things you have done well and, probably, have a target for you to work towards.

Other observations will be focused on your particular targets, either those identified before the placement or those identified at a mentor meeting. You may want a number of observations to address a particular target, such as giving appropriate praise, or using your voice effectively, or maintaining the pace of a lesson. Some of the targets will be designed to move your level of practice from a minimum standard to good or outstanding level. These focused observations will be particularly good for helping you to be aware of progress towards a particular standard.

Observation by your course tutor

If your ITT provider has course tutors who visit on placement, from another school, a teaching school alliance or university, they will usually observe you teaching. This will be the same sort of formal, written observation as your mentor makes and you will be given the notes and verbal feedback after the observation. The tutor will arrange a visit in advance and will probably ask to see a specific part of your teaching – a particular subject, or teaching in the outdoor classroom. The tutor will want to meet your mentor and class teacher and this might influence the timing of the visit. Tutors will usually arrive slightly earlier than the observation and try to put you at your ease by chatting informally for a few minutes. You should prepare as carefully for tutor observations as you would for a mentor observation. Have a copy of the lesson plan available for the tutor and make sure your placement file and training plan file are available if the tutor wants them. If you are in a Key Stage 1 or 2 class you should probably identify a place for the tutor to sit, so that he or she does not get in the way of the lesson. These details present you as a well organised professional even before your lesson is observed.

The course tutor may well do a joint observation with your mentor, class teacher or head teacher. This means they will both observe you at the same time, with the tutor and mentor making observation notes. Both observers will then discuss the observation between themselves before giving you feedback, including the written notes. The point of an observation like this is to ensure that both the mentor and the course tutor have the same expectations about your performance and that both make the same judgements about your teaching. This is a form of moderation and helps to ensure that all trainees are judged fairly.

MINI CASE MINI CASE MINI CASE **MINI CASE** MINI CASE MINI CASE **MINI CASE**

Tutor observations are nerve wracking because you don't really know the tutor that well. I was always secretly slightly concerned in case I was different from all the other trainees and just didn't know it!

Ben, SCITT Partnership (PGCE) trainee

My tutors were really helpful. They always gave feedback on my plans as well as the sessions. Most of the sessions where I have been observed went really well but one; when I did a Chinese New Year activity with a Reception group, it was a bit of a management disaster. I hadn't really considered that all the glittery things and gold paint would be so exciting for the children. They got a bit giddy and I didn't calm them down. I felt stressed and nervous and panicked a bit and the whole activity was disorganised, with overexcited children and me totally failing to use my key vocabulary or address my teaching objectives. I thought the tutor would be really cross and that I'd totally humiliated myself. Actually, she was fine. She did agree with my evaluation of the lesson (and it was painful to see that in writing) but she was very constructive. We identified a list of things to do to reduce my nervousness and to ensure I managed Foundation Key Stage groups better. Most importantly, my tutor pointed out that not every lesson is going to go well and that sometimes, a disaster might just be the session that is observed. It didn't affect my assessment because other lessons observed were good and the tutor could see from the lesson observation sheets in my file that my mentor had observed good sessions.

Gina, Early Years PGCE (part time)

Observation by your subject specialist or head teacher

These sessions will be formal written observations like those with your mentor. It is very useful to have a particular subject co-ordinator or phase co-ordinator look at their area of interest, especially if it is one of your target areas. Their expertise in the subject and also of observing other teachers' lessons will mean they can give you good feedback and new ideas. Prepare for these observations as you would for a mentor observation and make sure your plan is available to the observer.

Observation by moderators, external or internal examiners

All training programmes that offer an award such as a PGCE or BA have examiners of some sort. Internal examiners or moderators may be partnership staff or local head teachers who observe a number of trainees for moderation purposes. They will be observing to check that the expectations and judgements made by mentors and course tutors are consistent for all the trainees.

External examiners will be senior staff from other training partnerships. They perform a similar moderation role on most courses. They observe to ensure that the Teachers'

Standards are being met and that the grades awarded to trainees are consistent, not only across the course but for trainees in other programmes. Although you might not welcome a visit from an examiner you should not worry. They are very experienced and their visits protect the standard of your award by ensuring that grades are fair.

There are a number of reasons why you might have visits from examiners. A proportion of PGCE and BA candidates, where the award of the qualification is made by a university, are likely to have an external examiner visit towards the end of their final placement, whether or not they are in a SCITT partnership, as part of their programme. On an ITT course the most likely reason for a visit is that you have been chosen more or less at random as part of a sample of the cohort. However, if you have experienced severe difficulties and may not achieve the Standards for QTS, then you may also have a visit from the external examiner to collect evidence to inform an examination board. This evidence will be an important part of making the decision about whether you have met the Teachers' Standards.

Any visit by an external or internal examiner or moderator will be arranged in advance. They will expect to observe you teaching, talk to you, talk to your mentor or class teacher and look through your placement file and training plan. Make sure these are readily available and that you have a copy of your lesson plan ready to give your visitor. The examiner may give you feedback but you should not automatically expect detailed feedback if the main purpose of the visit is moderation. Remember, examiners will be as concerned to check that your assessors are making the right decisions as to make assessments of you.

Observation by Ofsted inspectors

You may be observed by Ofsted inspectors for two reasons. All ITT provision undergoes Ofsted inspection and so it is possible that you will be observed as part of the inspection of your ITT provider. In this case, you will be notified in advance and the partnership will tell you very clearly what to expect and what you should prepare. The inspector may want to observe you teaching, interview you and the mentor and take a detailed look at your files. Alternatively, the inspector might ask to observe another aspect of training, such as one of your mentor meetings. If you are notified of an Ofsted visit, contact your ITT provider, who will be able to tell you exactly what to expect, how long it will take and who will be involved. Your role is to ensure you are well prepared so that you are organised, professional and confident on the day. It would be unusual for inspectors to give detailed or written feedback after a visit to a trainee but they will usually give some, limited, verbal comments.

You might also be observed as part of the school's Ofsted inspection. As schools receive short notice of an inspection, an inspection week could well happen during your school based training. In this case the school will usually advise you about what they would like you to do that week. It is a good time to fit in and work together with the staff. Be prepared to support your teacher in any lessons that are observed or to be observed teaching yourself. Your teaching might well be confined to groups during Ofsted week, if your teacher prefers that. Be well prepared for whatever you teach and ensure your files are available. The inspector may want to talk to you about your experience in the school. Remember that, while you are not going to be the school's first priority during inspection week, Ofsted will be looking at the provision made for trainees by the school.

Ofsted inspectors will always talk to you if they observe you teaching, but you should not expect written feedback or much detail. Having an Ofsted inspection during your placement is a useful experience. You see the school at its best (well prepared) and its worst (nervous teachers). Being part of a school's Ofsted inspection teaches you that inspection is a routine part of school life – and experience of an Ofsted inspection is a great thing to talk about at job interviews.

Target-setting for your training

Throughout your training (and afterwards in your NQT year) you will be expected to set clear targets to help you improve your performance towards all aspects of the Teachers' Standards. Target-setting alone will not bring about improvement – it needs to lead to action. This section will help you to set realistic and demanding targets and to think through how your targets can be achieved through effective action.

Reviewing

In order to set your targets for each block of school experience you will need to review and analyse your current performance. Before you start school experience, your mentor or tutors will help you to set appropriate targets based on some general starting expectations taking into account your views of your previous experience. For example, on first placement, a trainee teacher who has been an experienced nursery nurse might be expected to address that part of Teachers' Standards, Part One, 8 which requires her to 'deploy support staff effectively' and work collaboratively with teaching assistants in a Nursery placement, whereas this would be far more challenging for a trainee coming straight from university and going into a Key Stage 2 placement.

If you are setting targets for your second or third block of school based training, you will start by reviewing the outcomes of your training so far. With your mentor or your course tutor, you will discuss your mentor's report from the previous term or placement, your observation notes, your teaching file and your own self-evaluation to identify your progress and needs. This is not to say that the beginning and end of placements are the only times to review your progress, but these are times when you are particularly concerned to set targets.

Progress with The Standards

An essential part of your programme is to achieve all of the Teachers' Standards. Therefore, during and after each school placement, it will be necessary for you to consider your progress against the particular standards related to that work. Mentors and course tutors will discuss school placements with you.

When considering standards you should:

- **know which standards you aimed to address during this placement;**
- **look at written feedback related to The Standards, e.g. placement reports, mentor meeting notes, observations;**
- **note oral feedback from mentors and tutors;**
- **get in mind what improving your performance relative to a particular standard looks like.**

There will be some standards you have not had the opportunity to address (perhaps because you were not in an appropriate age phase or situation) and some that you have not succeeded in demonstrating yet. These would be good candidates for your list of targets to be identified.

One way to consider how you can improve is to look at a grid like the UCET/NASBITT grid, which present descriptions so that you can see what minimum, good and outstanding performance, for a trainee on the point of qualification, looks like. For example, Standard 7 is set out on the UCET and NASBITT (2012) grid to describe trainee achievement at minimum, good and outstanding levels.

Target-setting

The more precise you can be in stating what you want to achieve the easier it will be for mentors and tutors to help you and for you to measure your achievement. Get a clear picture in your mind of what success in achieving your targets will look like by being able to complete the sentence 'I will know I have achieved this target when ...'.

Finally, set a realistic number of targets at the beginning of a placement and expect that some of them will be ticked off and replaced with new targets during the placement. Others will last for the duration of the placement and be more fully reviewed at the end of the placement. At the end of this placement, you should again review your progress and begin target-setting for your next placement.

MINI CASE MINI CASE MINI CASE **MINI CASE** MINI CASE MINI CASE **MINI CASE**

Louise had just completed her second school placement during which she had been placed with a Year 5 class. The placement had gone well and during her time in school she had progressed from taking parts of whole-class lessons or group work to sustained periods of whole-class teaching in some curriculum areas. Although she had had to develop a range of behaviour management strategies in order to promote purposeful learning environments, her mentor reported that Louise was sensitive to the needs of her class, demonstrated and promoted positive values and set high expectations. She had developed a pleasant relationship with the children.

Louise's mentor suggested that her targets included:

- 'Have high expectations of behaviour, and establish a framework for discipline with a range of strategies, using praise, sanctions and rewards consistently and fairly' (part of Teaching Standard 7).
- 'Communicate effectively with parents with regard to pupils' achievements and well-being' (part of Teaching Standard 8).

Louise understood that her pupils' attitudes and behaviour are influenced as much by their everyday lives outside school as by the time spent in school. Encouragement, support and guidance from both home and school are crucial and can have a significant impact on their learning. Louise appreciated the need for establishing a purposeful learning environment and that she needed a greater range of strategies in order to ensure that her pupils were always interested, motivated and remained on task.

This would help them to learn effectively, not disrupt others and make significant progress. In order to achieve the targets suggested, Louise began to make them more specific.

She arranged focused observations of experienced teachers in order to see how they dealt with specific aspects of behaviour management – settling children at the start of lessons, grouping children for practical activities, managing transitions between phases of the lesson, maintaining a brisk pace, using the voice effectively, using praise and encouragement, asking questions, intervening when children stray off task. She decided to talk through the school's behaviour policy with her mentor at the beginning of her next placement.

When dealing with parents, Louise decided to become proactive and talk informally with parents collecting their children from school. She decided to ask if she could write trial reports on some pupils and compare her efforts with those of her class teacher. She determined to talk to her mentor about how the school dealt with problems that necessitated formal discussions with parents. She looked forward to attending her first parents' evening.

Finally, at the end of your course, following your final placement in school, you must meet target-setting requirements for your NQT year. These can be:

- **areas of the standards where you have had little experience (such as a particular foundation subject you have not taught), work in the outdoor classroom or developing your expertise in working with parents;**
- **areas of the standards you found challenging throughout your ITT and want to strengthen, such as behaviour management or the way you use your voice;**
- **areas of interest to you, such as your specialist subject or special needs.**

Mentor meetings, professional relationships and advice

Some of the most important times in your training are your mentor meetings. These review progress, refocus your targets and maintain your progress towards achieving The Standards. It is very important that you agree a convenient, regular time and place for these at the start of your placement. You will also want to keep a record of your mentor meetings as evidence of your professional development, the actions you have taken to meet targets and progress in setting new targets. Some courses provide a special form for this (see Figure 7.1), but you can use ordinary paper or a word processor. Agree with your mentor who will take the notes and check you agree about what is recorded before you conclude the meeting.

When you begin a block of school based training you will have a set of expectations for that experience. It is important to ensure that you keep these, and your personal targets, in mind. One way to do this is to work out a rough timetable of mentor agenda items. You will not use them all but it means that you will not get to the end of the placement and suddenly find that you have three days left to do all your school based tasks, look at the school PHSE policy and teach RE.

Log of BA/PGCE/SCITT Trainee–Mentor Meeting This record should be maintained by the trainee and signed by both participants. A copy should go in the teaching file and the mentor's training file.		
Date: 20 June 2014	Trainee: Belinda Noyes, PGCE Mentor: June Smith	St Joseph's Primary School, Y1

Focus for discussion: The science observation done this week Changes to SEND arrangements in schools School-based tasks
Summary of discussion: The science observation identified differentiation for the most and least able as something to work on but showed progress in organising resources and managing the children. We talked about the upcoming Book Week and what costume I might try. We discussed the children in my class who have SEN and how I can incorporate some of the main needs identified for these children into my lesson plans. One of my school tasks is to examine the interventions in place in school.
Action points (referenced to the standards): Meet Mrs James (SENCO) to look at the planning for interventions in KS1, SEN targets for the children in my class and and review some of my lesson plans. June to organize. *TS5 (2) 5.* *know when and how to differentiate appropriately, using approaches which enable pupils to be taught effectively* *have a secure understanding of how a range of factors can inhibit pupils' ability to learn, and how best to overcome these* June will observe my literacy next week, looking at the differentiation. TS5 (3) *demonstrate an awareness of the physical, social and intellectual development of children, and know how to adapt teaching to support pupils' education at different stages of development*
Signed (Mentor) ....   Signed (Trainee) ....

Figure 7.1 Sample mentor meeting notes

On her second school based training block of five weeks, Belinda's planned agendas looked like this (see Figure 7.2):

Week	Routine items	Things I want to focus on if other issues do not arise
1	The requirements for the block of school based training. My personal targets. School welcome pack. What I will observe this week, and my first teaching experiences.	The behaviour policy. School SEN policy.
2	My observations so far of core subjects. Plan to get school tasks (pupil profiles) done.	My teaching of group guided reading and the mathematics structure.
3	No meeting.	
4	Observations of my teaching in the last fortnight. Progress on school tasks (observing administration of Phonics screening test).	Review of needs of SEND children in my class, meeting with the SENCO.
5	Observations of me teaching this week. Concluding school tasks (discuss marking of National Tests).	Discuss my teaching report. Have self-evaluation prepared.

Figure 7.2 Agenda items

Assessment of your school based training

Your school based training will be assessed against the Teachers' Standards. Each placement may have different requirements and not every standard will be assessed in each teaching situation, so it is important you are aware of which standards will be assessed during your particular block of training.

For a shorter block of school based training, your mentor will usually write a report towards the end of the block. The format of this varies from course to course, but you will usually be assessed against each section of the Teachers' Standards and comments will be made about your progress in each area:

PREAMBLE

PART ONE: TEACHING

1 Set high expectations which inspire, motivate and challenge pupils

2 Promote good progress and outcomes by pupils

3 Demonstrate good subject and curriculum knowledge

4 Plan and teach well structured lessons

5 Adapt teaching to respond to the strengths and needs of all pupils

6 Make accurate and productive use of assessment

7 Manage behaviour effectively to ensure a good and safe learning environment

8 Fulfil wider professional responsibilities

PART TWO: PERSONAL AND PROFESSIONAL CONDUCT

A teacher is expected to demonstrate consistently high standards of personal and professional conduct.

You may be graded against each section of the standards or against each standard. The grades will usually be:

1. **Excellent**
2. **Good**
3. **Requires improvement**
4. **Unsatisfactory.**

Each course will have a slightly different format and grading system, so be sure to review the assessment forms and criteria early in your school based training. Examples are provided below, but they may be slightly different from those on your training course. School based training reports will usually be word processed but some partnerships may write them.

You may well have an interim report in the middle of the school based training block, perhaps around half term if you are in your base school. This supplements the meetings you have with your mentor and ensures you review your progress in good time and revise any targets you need. If there are any areas for serious concern, you will be aware of them and can work with your mentor to address them.

These interim and final reports (also called profiles or assessments) will form a valuable part of your training plan as they are evidence that you have addressed certain standards.

The assessment of your school based training will be evidence based. The sources of evidence will be the formal observations of your teaching made during the placement, discussion with your class teacher about what he or she has observed, records of mentor meetings and evidence you have collected in your placement file, including lesson plans, assessment records, mock reports and school tasks.

Extract from a school based training report

Term 1

Jenny Xi, Year 5

Attendance   satisfactory   unsatisfactory

Jenny has been on time and well prepared for her teaching, in terms of doing plans and reviewing pupil performance in lessons.

General comment

Jenny made a difficult start. She found it hard to manage the class and to establish an appropriate working relationship but she was very tenacious and never gave up.

Table 7.1

A teacher must:				
	4 Requires improvement	3 Minimum standard	2 Good	1 Outstanding
1 Sets high expectations which inspire, motivate and challenge pupils		x		
2 Promotes good progress and outcomes by pupils		X		
3 Demonstrates good subject and curriculum knowledge		X		
4 Plans and teaches well-structured lessons		x		
5 Adapt teaching to respond to the strengths and needs of all pupils			X	
6 Make accurate and productive use of assessment		X		
7 Manage behaviour effectively to ensure a good and safe learning environment		x		
8 Fulfil wider professional responsibilities			X	

She has taken the advice offered by her tutor, mentor and class teacher about the strategies for promoting positive behaviour. As a result, she made real progress with classroom management. By the last week she had achieved a calm, working ethos and the children listened well in maths and English sessions.

Teaching

Main areas of strength in teaching

Jenny worked hard to improve her teaching by taking advice and acting on it and forged a good professional relationship with her class teacher and mentor, though she is not yet connected to the rest of the staff (Teachers' Standards, Preamble). Although she was reticent in her manner and very quiet with other teachers, Jenny did gain confidence as the placement developed. She was consistently thoughtful about pupils and had begun to recognise their needs (2.2) and adapt the teaching objectives in response to their performance on previous lessons (in English and maths) (5.2).

In maths and English her subject knowledge was good and she took the phonics group independently for the last week of the term (3.1, 3.4).

Targets for teaching

Jenny needs the opportunity to make contact with parents and carers and find out about the mechanisms for reporting to them because she has not had a chance to do this. Jenny now needs to develop her evaluation of pupils in lessons into more systematic assessment (TS6.1).

Jenny has made good progress with TS7 but now needs to do this in another class to develop confidence.

Using your school based training report

When you have your school based training report you can use it to set specific targets for your next placement, as evidence towards the completion of the Teachers' Standards and to inform your completion of the Career Entry and Development Profile. To do this, you will review the evidence of your report, lesson plans, assessment records and observations of your teaching against the criteria or descriptions of what each standard looks like. You can use descriptors from your course materials or the UCET/NASBITT grid identified earlier.

MINI CASE MINI CASE MINI CASE **MINI CASE** MINI CASE MINI CASE **MINI CASE**

Keisha had completed her first term with a Year 4 class. During her first term in school she had progressed from taking parts of whole-class lessons or group work to sustained periods of whole-class teaching in English and maths. Although she had had been evaluating her lessons in terms of children's learning, she felt she had not begun to understand assessment. In discussion with her mentor, Keisha suggested that it was time for her to learn more about assessment and address aspects of Teachers' Standards, Part One, 6:

6. Make accurate and productive use of assessment.

(Continued)

(Continued)

Table 7.2

6 Make accurate and productive use of assessment	By the end of the programme of ITE, all those trainees recommended for the award of QTS will have demonstrated that:	Those trainees graded as 'good' at the end of the programme of ITE may have demonstrated additionally that:	Those trainees graded as 'outstanding' at the end of the programme of ITE may have demonstrated additionally that:
-know and understand how to assess the relevant subject and curriculum areas, including statutory assessment requirements -make use of formative and summative assessment to secure pupils' progress -use relevant data to monitor progress, set targets, and plan subsequent lessons -give pupils regular feedback, both orally and through accurate marking, and encourage pupils to respond to the feedback.	They have a secure understanding of the statutory assessment requirements for the subject / curriculum in the age phases they are preparing to teach and are able to make broadly accurate assessments against national benchmarks. Their planning is characterised by the use of a range of formative and summative assessment strategies, designed to support pupils in making progress. They deploy these strategies effectively in lessons, both to evaluate the impact of teaching on the progress of learners and as a basis for modifying their teaching and classroom practice when necessary. They understand how school and pupil level summative data is used to set targets for groups and individuals and they use that knowledge to monitor progress in the groups they teach. With guidance from experienced teachers, they monitor pupil progress and maintain accurate records, setting new targets for individuals and groups. They mark pupils' work constructively and provide appropriate oral feedback to pupils to help them to make progress.	They are able to assess pupils' attainment accurately against national benchmarks. They employ a range of appropriate formative assessment strategies effectively and can adapt their teaching within lessons in light of pupils' responses. They maintain accurate records of pupils' progress and use these to set appropriately challenging targets. They assess learners' progress regularly and accurately and discuss assessments with them so that learners know how well they have done and what they need to do to improve.	They can confidently and accurately assess pupils' attainment against national benchmarks. They use a range of assessment strategies very effectively in their day to day practice to monitor progress and to inform future planning. They systematically and effectively check learners' understanding throughout lessons, anticipating where intervention may be needed and do so with notable impact on the quality of learning. They assess learners' progress regularly and work with them to accurately target further improvement and secure rapid progress.

- **know and understand how to assess the relevant subject and curriculum areas, including statutory assessment requirements;**
- **make use of formative and summative assessment to secure pupils' progress.**

Keisha understood that assessment was happening in every lesson and should affect her planning and also that there were some high-stakes tests which she was somewhat hazy about. So, she set herself targets for her Y4 class and then for the Y1 placement she would undertake later in the year.

She planned a general target: to learn about the high stakes tests in KS 1 and 2 and the school system for tracking pupil progress, and added specific actions.

- **Talk to the assessment coordinator in her home (junior) school, about school practices;**
- **Research KS1 and 2 statutory tests and tasks on the internet, starting with the DfE websites;**
- **Plan a meeting with her Y4 class teacher to follow through the year's tracking of pupils in her class;**
- **Watch a Teachers' TV programme about administration of KS2 tests;**
- **Plan a meeting with her KS1 class teacher to discuss the tracking of progress in maths, English and phonics;**
- **Observe and take part in the administration of the KS1 phonics screening test.**

At the end of her second term, Keisha completed all these actions and had notes and a positive placement report from her KS1 placement. She felt she had made progress on Standard 6 and on her grid of standards, she evaluated her Standard 6 in this way.

Though Keisha has more to do, with this evaluation of her progress she can now pick out what she has to do to improve.

Problems during your school based training

In one sense, all school based training present problems for you to solve. Education is, in itself, problematic and you, like the children, learn by setting yourself new tasks and problems. Unfortunately, sometimes difficulties can arise during school based training that threaten to affect your progress. The very best way to deal with problems is to prevent them arising. This is a matter of being very clear about your targets, your expectations, your course of training and what your school has to offer. You should also know who to go to in the case of difficulties and exactly what to do if you have to be absent from school for some reason. Read your course documentation carefully before you start your school based training and make sure you do this before you go into each of your schools.

Unfortunately, at some time during your placement you may feel that you have a problem or difficulty with it. If this happens to you there are a number of things you can do.

- **The most common areas for difficulties with school based training are the allocation of schools, relationships with class teachers, tutors or mentors, assessment of your progress and behaviour management in class. There are sections in this book you may find helpful with these issues. Read the relevant section and consider your problem against this background. A little more research may help you solve your problem.**
- **See any problem as a test of your ability to demonstrate your professional values and practice. This does not make any problem go away, but it does get you in the right frame of mind to solve it positively, and maintain good relationships.**

- Think carefully about whether you really do have a problem with your school based training. If the issue annoying you is a result of, perhaps, a comparison with a friend, you might be placing undue emphasis on a minor issue. Always consider this possibility. School based training is a very pressurised experience and some people respond excessively to minor irritations.
- You may have problems during school based training that are not directly caused by the training itself but affect it seriously – illness, bereavement, etc. Make sure you discuss these with your mentor and make the necessary arrangements. Life happens!
- If you feel there is a problem with your school based experience that is affecting your training, you should talk to your mentor about it in the first instance. Do not let a problem grumble on throughout your school based training without saying anything. If you do this you will have a miserable, resentful time – probably unnecessarily.
- Your mentor really is your first port of call to discuss problems during school based training. If you go straight to other members of staff or to the head teacher before consulting your mentor you could cause offence.
- When you raise a problem with your mentor, make sure you do it as a fellow professional. Make sure you do not accuse individuals, become overwrought or apportion blame. State clearly what your problem is and, if possible, suggest possible solutions or ask your mentor to help you identify possible actions. This shows you are really trying to seek a solution.
- Choose your time to raise a problem carefully. Avoid the temptation to share an important issue in passing during break or in the corridor. Instead you might arrange a brief meeting after school or wait for a mentor meeting.
- Your problem may be such that you cannot discuss it with your mentor. In this case you need to decide who to talk to. This depends on the structure of your training. If you have a course tutor this might be the person. If you are in a SCITT provider you should check who manages the provision. It is very important that you read your course documentation and talk to the right person – this may be a course tutor, personal tutor, SCITT manager or head teacher.
- If you choose to confide your problem to your class teacher make sure you are thoughtful and professional in the way you do so.
- Whoever you discuss your problem with will treat it confidentially and professionally. You must do the same within school.
- If you feel your problem is serious and you have not been able to resolve it with your mentor and course tutor you should write to your course leader and ask him or her to help you solve the problem.
- Finally, and this really is if all else has failed, your course will have a complaints procedure. You can use this if you feel you have been unfairly treated.
- Accept that schools are not perfect and be prepared to make an effort to resolve problems. Never give up because you have encountered difficulty. Look for ways to get around it.
- Never, never, never just walk out of school based training, whatever you feel. This is always unjustifiable, unprofessional behaviour.
- Congratulate yourself when you are able to resolve problems effectively. This is a real professional skill.

Sorting out problems during your school based training is a test of your resilience. If you can deal with your difficulties well you will avoid strain and be able to continue your training purposefully.

REFLECTIVE TASK

Identify one target for improvement in your professional skills: planning, teaching, assessing, reviewing, learning environment or team work. This target may be one of your key priorities for your first experience of school based training or a target arising from a previous experience. An example might be 'have high expectations of behaviour, and establish a framework for discipline with a range of strategies, using praise, sanctions and rewards consistently and fairly' (Teaching Standard 7).

Review the following issues in relation to your target.

- **What is already in place in your setting? (Behaviour policy, observe the teacher to see what he/she does.)**

- **What you know about frameworks for classroom discipline. (http://www.behaviour2learn. co.uk/)**

- **What opportunities you have identified to work on in this target. (First whole-class session, group support work.)**

- **What feedback you can get about your target. (Will your teacher or mentor observe?)**

A SUMMARY OF KEY POINTS

- Each trainee's training is different because each trainee is different. Placements are chosen to meet your training needs.

- As you go through your ITT you will compile a training plan (or record of professional development). This will include your achievements and targets. Your targets will help you to address the Teachers' Standards.

- To make the most of your school based training you must be sure you know what the requirements are and what your targets are. You can then plan to achieve them.

- Your mentor is an important person in your training. He or she will help you to set and monitor targets and arrange training experiences. Your mentor will be involved in your assessment. Mentor meetings are a key training experience and to use them well you should be prepared and keep records of meetings and agreed targets.

- You will be observed teaching on placement by a number of people. Make sure you know why you are being observed and prepare well for your observation.

- Your mentor, class teacher and course tutor may be involved in your assessment. Make sure they have evidence of your achievements and can easily look at your training plan and teaching file.

- Your assessment report is an important document and you will use it as evidence towards The Standards and to set targets for future teaching and professional development.

- Professional problems can be sorted out in a professional way. Deal with any problems swiftly and positively so that you can move on and get the most from your placement.

RESOURCES RESOURCES **RESOURCES** RESOURCES **RESOURCES** **RESOURCES**

Full details of the Teachers' Standards are given on the DfE website at: https://www.gov.uk/government/publications/teachers-standards

Further information about the implementation and use of the Teachers' Standards can be found on a number of local websites, including that maintained by The Borough of Kensington and Chelsea: http://www.rbkc.gov.uk/educationandlearning/cpdforschools/newlyqualifiedteachers/nqtinductionhandbook/theprofessionalstandards.aspx

Teacher support line: http://teachersupport.info/get-support/phone

This is a confidential national 24-hour telephone counselling, support and advice service for teachers, run by the Teacher Support Network. Free to all teacher trainees and teachers in Primary and Secondary schools in England, Scotland and Wales. You can now access counselling using email through the website. Simply follow the links from the homepage. Telephone 08000 562 561 or visit www.teachersupport.info.

8
The challenges of school based training

Learning outcomes

As your training proceeds you will find some aspects more challenging than others. In this chapter we address some of the significant areas of professional activity on school based training. By the end of this chapter you should:

- **know how to prepare for working well with other adults;**
- **know some strategies for managing children's behaviour;**
- **know what to do if you encounter a child protection issue.**

Working with other adults

Some of the Teachers' Standards deal with working with other adults. You will need to demonstrate that you:

○ *make a positive contribution to the wider life and ethos of the school*

○ *develop effective professional relationships with colleagues, knowing how and when to draw on advice and specialist support*

○ *deploy support staff effectively.*

(Teachers' Standards, Part One, 8: Fulfil wider professional responsibilities)

On school based training you will be working with a range of other adults. They may include adults who do not teach but are extremely valuable members of staff:

- **school secretaries or administrators;**
- **lunchtime supervisors;**
- **school caretakers;**
- **before or after school carers or club managers;**
- **non-teacher coaching or teaching staff.**

You need to find out about the roles of these members of staff and how they affect you. It is important that you establish a similar relationship with them as you have with your teacher, so you need to know details. For instance, how does the school administrator manage the lunch money? How are registers sent to the secretary? How should you manage the transition to lunchtime/after school activities? How do you manage the transition to netball coaching time? What do you have to do to ensure these practices are maintained?

Another category of adults will work with you in the classroom or setting. These will include:

- Early Years practitioners;
- teaching assistants;
- school teaching staff such as the SENCO, teachers from other parts of the school such as a behaviour, communication or learning unit, a special needs teaching assistant;
- visiting professionals such as psychologists, support teachers, social workers, etc.;
- parents.

Early Years practitioners

If you are undertaking a school based training in an Early Years setting such as an EYFS unit, a Nursery class or Reception class, nursery nurses, practitioners, assistants or facilitators will be part of your school based training. They will be part of the teaching team and you will usually do your planning together as a team. At first it may be difficult to identify the differences between the roles of the teacher and other practitioners. All will set up resources, plan activities, make assessment notes and take time out to observe children. All will manage behaviour, deal with incidents and talk to parents. However, the teacher will lead the planning and assessment and manage the overall situation. This is the role you are aiming for, so you too must learn to work well in a team. Practitioners may work as a full-time member of the teaching team or in one of the ways described below.

Teaching assistants

Teaching assistants have a vital role to play throughout the Primary phase and there are now more of them in the profession than ever before. Teaching assistants are deployed strategically to meet the needs of the school or particular pupils.

- **Some teaching assistants will work with a particular child, as a result of special needs provision and a school decision on action for this child. A teaching assistant may have a specific role for a child, or children, with EAL. The teaching assistant may work with the child during whole class work, to support their involvement and understanding, and then work with them in a group. The teaching assistant may also work with other children in the group. You will be expected to plan for the teaching assistant's involvement.**
- **Teaching assistants from a special unit may work with a child who is spending part of the time in the unit and part of the time in your class. In this case you will need to plan with the teaching assistant to ensure continuity and understanding.**
- **Some teaching assistants will spend all or part of their time working with a specific class, set or classes. This is a regular arrangement that allows you to plan for teaching assistant involvement and to obtain assessment evidence from the teaching assistants.**
- **Some higher level teaching assistants will supervise the class at agreed times when work has been set for the children and actual teaching is not demanded. They will not usually mark written work. You will need to learn to plan and set work, mark the results and handle the processes of handing over the class and obtaining feedback about what they have done.**
- **Some teaching assistants will manage and run particular programmes such as booster classes, reading recovery, catch-up or another intervention and support programme. These may be school based programmes and involve the teaching assistant in working both in your class, perhaps during the whole class part of the lesson, and with a specific group in or out of the class for group work. Alternatively the teaching assistant may take children out of class to a more suitable area. It is worth asking the teaching assistant to explain the programme to you and observing at least one of the sessions.**

- Teaching assistants may make and prepare resources for you and will put up displays but you must know how much time they have to do this and what demands are reasonable. You must ensure that you ask for resources in good time and do not expect instant miracles or make impossible demands.

As part of your induction you need to find out which teaching assistants work in your class and what their role is. You should do this by asking the teacher first of all, and it would also be useful to ask the teaching assistants to explain their role to you. You should ask:

- What teaching assistants or Early Years practitioners work in this class or setting?
- What is the role of each practitioner or teaching assistant?
- If the teaching assistant's role is with a particular child or children, how does this affect others they work with?
- Does the teaching assistant have special responsibility for SEND or EAL?
- When does each practitioner or teaching assistant work with this class or pupil?
- What role does the teaching assistant or practitioner take in planning and assessment?
- What role does the teaching assistant or practitioner take in different parts of the sessions? Do practitioners or teaching assistants lead whole class rhyme time, support individuals during whole class activities, work with groups or take groups of children out of the classroom?
- What will the teaching assistant/practitioner prepare? Some teaching assistants prepare all the activities for their intervention programme but most will expect to participate in putting out resources for some activities.

As you build up responsibility for planning sessions and sequences of lessons you will be working closely with other adults. In an Early Years setting this may mean agreeing to the outline planning for each activity and session but some of the detail will be planned by other practitioners. You will need to see this planning so that you know what is happening in the setting, as your teacher would do. In a Key Stage 1 or 2 class you will be planning for teaching assistants. When you are planning for someone else it is vital that you are very clear about what role you want them to play and what you want the children to learn – this is a basic professional role but it is not as simple as it sounds in a busy class. You cannot expect teaching assistants to read your mind and a very common mistake is to make assumptions about what a teaching assistant knows and fail to explain properly what is required. This puts the teaching assistant or practitioner in a difficult position and they may not be able to do what you want.

We recommend you use a planning format such as the one given in Chapter 4 to make sure that the learning objectives (or outcomes) of a lesson are clear, that the teaching assistant knows exactly what language to use, what support to offer and that he or she can record brief assessment information for you. Research has identified reasons why the practice of having teaching assistants in the classroom may not promote learning. One reason for a lack of effectiveness is poor communication with the teacher, probably because of lack of time. Many TAs have multiple roles and cannot spend time discussing sessions or feeding back on pupil achievement. This means they are not as effective as they could be.

Another reason why TAs may not promote improved learning is that some teaching assistants may help children to complete the activity, rather than addressing the learning objectives. This is why it is important to be clear about the learning objectives. Your teaching assistant may not be used to having a written plan for lessons but you want to make quite sure you are explicit and a planning sheet is one way to do this. Using a sheet like this is useful for all these reasons but it also has a training role for you. If you become used to planning in detail for a teaching assistant early in your career, you are more likely to continue to think through these issues, even when you do not use a planning sheet for teaching assistants.

You will find that many Early Years practitioners and teaching assistants you work with are well qualified and very experienced. This can feel intimidating when you are starting your school based training. However, experienced teaching assistants or practitioners are a real asset. You will benefit from working alongside them and learning from their expertise. You are training for a slightly different role, as teacher, and you are not competing with teaching assistants or practitioners. When working with teaching assistants or practitioners you have a responsibility to be professional, well organised and to behave confidently because to do otherwise undermines their work as well as your own.

MINI CASE MINI CASE MINI CASE MINI CASE MINI CASE MINI CASE MINI CASE

On my first school based training block in the Nursery unit everyone worked together. Each practitioner planned for one area of learning each week and managed a teacher-directed and a couple of child-led activities each session. We sort of discussed them at the Thursday meeting then planned our own. At first I thought everyone did exactly the same but after a couple of meetings I realised that Jill (the teacher) steered the planning and used the documents and records to plan. She was really leading the planning and also looking at everyone's plans on a Friday. I worked up to it and did it with her.

Sara, PGCE

I was a teaching assistant myself before this course so it has sometimes been strange doing teacher training. In my second school based training I had a full-time teaching assistant (Cath) in the Year 1 class. Actually I found planning for her a bit of a burden. I mean it was great having her. I did things I couldn't have done on my own and I know it improved the children's learning but there were days when I felt that planning for her was just the last straw. My own experience as a teaching assistant helped me to be clear about exactly what I wanted Cath to do and to make sure I talked with her before and after lessons. Even that, though, was something I had to practise. I found Cath very reassuring. She was positive and calm but when I was a teaching assistant myself, I never realised that working with a teaching assistant would be an effort.

Chloe, SCITT trainee

In my school there are 12 teaching assistants. Some are assigned to particular classes and some to particular children. Two of them are specially trained to do the intervention programmes for struggling children and work with groups outside the class. One of the teaching assistants is something of an expert on guided reading and does a lot of that in Key Stage 1, working in all the Year 1 classes. I worked with two of the teaching assistants, one (Ellie) in class supporting a child with autistic spectrum disorder and one (Nerika) who did guided reading. I planned for Ellie in all my lesson plans as a differentiation issue and so I asked her to look at my daily plans. She supported her child but also the whole group and it was important that they didn't depend on her too much and addressed the objectives themselves. With Nerika, I had to monitor the guided reading and get feedback from her. I found it quite difficult to suggest texts as she knew them better than me. I became confident working with Ellie and Nerika when I convinced myself that I had nothing to prove. Both teaching assistants were very supportive to me.

Jo, PGCE trainee

School teaching staff

Staff working alongside you in your class may include EAL teachers, the SEN co-ordinator and teachers from specialist units (such as behaviour support). You need to discuss their roles in much the same way as you would the teaching assistant's role. Make sure you know what they aim to do, which children they are targeting and how they work with you. This may mean that they observe and assess certain children that they support children in doing activities you are teaching or that they plan, in cooperation with you, for slightly different activities for the target children. Specialist teachers may also come into your class to advise you and help you differentiate for certain children.

Visiting professionals

Educational psychologists, curriculum support advisers and social workers may come to your class for a variety of reasons. Their visits may be part of a school policy implementation or there may be concern about particular children. You should discuss the role of each professional with your teacher and, where possible, shadow him/her at meetings in which they are involved. However, some meetings (for instance those about child protection issues) may be confidential and so sensitive that it would not be appropriate for you to attend. In this case you can still discuss the processes for this sort of meeting without discussing the content. Ensure you know the role of each visiting professional you encounter, how their involvement was triggered, how long they have been involved with the class or child and what the likely actions resulting from such involvement will be.

Parents

Parents may also work in your classroom voluntarily. They will not have had the sort of training or experience a teaching assistant has had, so it is doubly important to ensure you know their accustomed role and that you are very clear about what you would like them to do. In some cases parents come in to work on a particular school initiative, such as a story sack project in the Early Years Foundation Stage or a talking book project with juniors. Find out about these initiatives. In other cases parents come in to assist with a certain lesson. For instance, a parent might come in on one morning a week to play the guitar for the class music session or to supervise handwriting with groups of children. Having parents in classes carries certain child protection and confidentiality issues and all parents coming into class will complete a criminal record disclosure process and have a discussion with a member of school staff about maintaining confidentiality.

Management of children's behaviour

Managing the behaviour of the children in your class is a key issue. You need to demonstrate that you can: 'Manage behaviour effectively to ensure a good and safe learning environment' (Teachers' Standards, Part One, 7). In order to do this you will need to:

- **have clear rules and routines for behaviour in classrooms, and take responsibility for promoting good and courteous behaviour both in classrooms and around the school, in accordance with the school's behaviour policy;**
- **have high expectations of behaviour, and establish a framework for discipline with a range of strategies, using praise, sanctions and rewards consistently and fairly;**

- manage classes effectively, using approaches which are appropriate to pupils' needs in order to involve and motivate them;
- maintain good relationships with pupils, exercise appropriate authority, and act decisively when necessary.

These issues are the bedrock of good teaching because you simply cannot teach successfully if the class is unruly, will not pay attention to you and is not interested in what you are doing.

The school behaviour policy

The first document of interest to you in a new school is the school behaviour policy. This sets out the school's aims in terms of the ethos and behaviour of the school and the sort of relationships the staff want to establish. It also sets out the strategies that are used, consistently and by all teachers, to establish and maintain a positive ethos and good relationships. Read this document as soon as possible and observe how your teacher implements the rewards and sanctions described in the policy.

Establishing expectations – the class teacher contract

You will undertake your school based training in a class or setting run by a successful teacher. The class will be well behaved and working successfully, but each class will be slightly different. For a start, each teacher establishes different expectations of the children at the start of the year and enforces these. This is how the children recognise what is acceptable and learn exactly what is not acceptable. Some teachers will explicitly negotiate rules for acceptable behaviour at the beginning of the year, display these on the wall and review them periodically. This is useful because it gives the teacher a chance to discuss rules positively and make clear the point of each rule, such as 'Talk quietly so that others can be heard' rather than 'No shouting'. However, all teachers have an unspoken contract with their class that ensures that the children behave well as long as they are engaged and interested. If either the teacher or children fail to deliver their part of the contract, the balance of good behaviour may break down.

PRACTICAL TASK PRACTICAL TASK PRACTICAL TASK PRACTICAL TASK PRACTICAL TASK

Observe your class to ensure you know the terms of the unwritten contract between teacher and children – the expectations, rules and sanctions used on a daily basis. Use the questions below as guidance.

- **What are the rules for talking in a session/lesson?**
- **How do children know when to pay attention to the teacher talking?**
- **How does the teacher know when children are bored or not understanding work?**
- **What are the rules about taking turns in talking during a group or class meeting?**
- **What are the rules for moving around the class?**
- **What are the rules for going out of the class during a session/lesson?**
- **What are the rules for moving equipment around?**

Watch the teacher teaching and try to work out the scale of sanctions and rewards in the class. How does the teacher reward good attention or performance? Identify the rewards your teacher uses that you will need to add to the list. Rewards might be:

- **making eye contact with the child;**
- **making eye contact and smiling;**
- **making eye contact and nodding or other gestures;**
- **using verbal rewards (praise) – 'Well done', 'Good', 'Spot on', 'Lovely', etc.;**
- **using small physical gestures such as patting an arm when praising;**
- **giving a token reward – a house point or sticker (these may add up to a larger reward in a school system);**
- **drawing the rest of the class or group's attention to good behaviour or work – 'Look at Ben's great picture!';**
- **putting a reward sticker or points on to a class chart;**
- **earning 'golden time' or some other privilege;**
- **sending the child to some higher authority to show good work (such as the deputy head);**
- **mentioning or rewarding good behaviour in a key stage or class assembly.**

Each time the teacher uses one of these rewards, as he or she does hundreds of times a day, it ensures that the behaviour that was praised or rewarded is more likely to occur again.

What does the teacher do when a child does not meet the expectations of the teacher in terms of behaviour? Here are some sanctions:

- **making eye contact with the child;**
- **making eye contact and frowning;**
- **making eye contact and nodding or other gestures;**
- **using the name of a child who is misbehaving to get their attention;**
- **using verbal sanctions – 'Please don't', 'Not now', etc.;**
- **not giving a token reward – a house point or sticker;**
- **giving a token punishment such as writing the child's name on the board (there will usually be a system of how many names are acceptable in a day);**
- **spending a minute or so away from activities (time out);**
- **drawing the rest of the class or group's attention to poor behaviour or work – 'What should Ben do?';**
- **taking a child aside for a quiet word about unacceptable behaviour;**
- **keeping a child in class during playtime;**
- **sending the child to some higher authority to prevent disruption (such as the deputy head – but never send a child out of the class unaccompanied);**
- **calling another teacher to come and fetch a child.**

When you observe your teacher, take about 20 minutes to keep a tally of how many rewards are given out (tiny little things like a brief smile, word or a gesture) and how many sanctions are used. You will

(Continued)

(Continued)

invariably find that many more rewards are used than sanctions. This is called 'catching them being good'. If you find yourself beginning to nag at children, continually criticise or keep repeating the same names you need to check whether you are being very negative. This will not change behaviour. Start to scan the class routinely every minute or so and catch someone being good. The reward of a smile, a nod or a well-chosen word does more to establish good behaviour than nagging.

The list of rules, rewards and sanctions you compile is essential knowledge in any class if you are to step into the teacher's shoes.

Acting like a teacher – your part of the contract

As a trainee you want the children to see you as the teacher and respect you as a teacher. Children are certainly not afraid of their teachers so why do they respect and behave well for them? Firstly, because teachers act like teachers, sending out all sorts of subtle signals that indicate they know what they are doing, have authority and expect children to behave well. You need to send out these signals if you want the children to recognise your authority. Here are some strategies for acting like the teacher in a class or Early Years setting.

- **Know the children by name.** If you know names you have a good start. 'Please sit down, Jamie' is so much more authoritative than 'Please sit down, no, not you, you'. If necessary label children with stickers with their names on. Thank and praise children by name, too.
- **Look like a teacher** – this does not mean a new wardrobe, just sensible choices that show you recognise the dress code in the school and fit into the teacher category of adults.
- **Move confidently and avoid skulking in the background.** If you are feeling nervous, stand up so the children can see you, rather than sitting down.
- **Use your voice confidently.** Your voice is your best tool and needs to vary in pace, tone, pitch and volume. The children respond to changes in your voice, not shouting. So sometimes dropping your voice to a whisper attracts attention better than shouting.
- **Make sure you have a signal for getting the attention of the whole class.** If your teacher uses clapping, hands in the air or a tambourine, you should start by using that signal even if it is not really your style. Everyone develops their own attention-grabbing signal eventually. Some teachers say 'OK, right!', 'Children!', 'Listen, please'; some snap their fingers, clap and sing to get attention. You may not find out what your personal signal is until you hear the children imitating you. All are effective when used confidently.
- **Do not begin to talk to the class or group until they are silent.** Wait, even if it seems to take ages. If you talk while the children are talking it signals that it is acceptable to ignore you and that you are not a real teacher.
- **Know the systems in the class or setting.** If you do not know something make sure you ask the children to tell you in a confident manner. 'Jennie, please put this buggy away where it belongs' is confident. 'I'm not sure where these go – do you know?' is not.
- **Use eye contact, without staring, as a way to engage, interest and bring children back on task.**
- **Have a range of facial expression, ranging from a relaxed, open smile to a frown or shocked look.**
- **Follow the children's established routine and make it clear you know what happens and what you expect.**

- Maintain the same expectations about behaviour as the teacher (you will have observed these very carefully).
- Scan the class so that you can spot (and reward) good behaviour and keep an eye out for those misbehaving or children who are off task. Developing this scanning involves looking up and around at regular intervals. It is known as teacher radar.
- Act purposefully. Know what you are doing and get on with it. Going straight into what you have planned engages interest and prevents disruption.
- Prepare interesting, relevant lessons that everyone can participate in. This is, of course, the big challenge but it is the child who is bored, left out, struggling or clueless who shows inappropriate behaviour – and becomes your nightmare.
- Be prepared for the unexpected. If you are ever in a situation where you do not know what to do, then do something purposeful – a few action rhymes, a bit of times tables practice, a team quiz or reading some poems can fill most gaps without undermining your authority. You should always have some emergency filler like this ready.

These sorts of strategies make your authority and your role as the teacher clear. However, you must also be aware of the ways in which you can step out of role and lose control. Do *not*, therefore:

- Plan work they cannot do, do not understand or find boring.
- Fail to explain what you want and they should do, so that they are confused.
- Waste their time by not getting down to things at once.
- Try to use inducements or rewards in an attempt to be liked.
- Beg feebly, rather than telling: 'Will you . . .?' can be answered with 'No!'. 'Please ...' cannot.
- Enter into arguments with children. You know best because you are the teacher – never argue with a child.
- Overpraise everything so that your praise has no meaning.
- Ignore or not recognise bad behaviour that should be dealt with.
- Use sarcasm or irony that the children cannot understand or make jokes at their expense.
- Act inconsistently or unfairly.
- Fail to distinguish yourself – children need to engage with your character through your voice and gestures: this is often what makes lessons interesting.

MINI CASE MINI CASE MINI CASE **MINI CASE** MINI CASE MINI CASE **MINI CASE**

In my first school I was nervous. I really didn't want to seem like a know-all in front of my teacher or other students. I made the classic mistake of being too equivocal and not establishing myself as a teacher. I asked them to do things then didn't follow up if they ignored me and I couldn't get them all quiet at once. The children sussed my nerves at once and were really rowdy. I couldn't understand it at all. They were angels for Jean (the teacher) and devils for me. After a week or so Jean and my mentor sat me down and talked it through. We came up with a plan. My first aim was to get them quiet and set a simple task. I would not talk over them but I would really act, so that my voice was much more colourful. It was terrifying the first time. I had to name some naughty ones and get Jean to sit with them but I did it. I worked on using my voice, radiating authority and getting them quiet all school based training. It was my hardest and most important lesson but I can honestly say it has not been an issue since

Niki, BA student

(Continued)

(Continued)

I was told on my course 'Don't smile until Christmas', a humorous way of saying that you need to establish your authority before you can have a warm relationship. But it didn't stop me getting it wrong. I was too friendly and let the children in the nursery treat me differently to the other staff. They would put their hands in my pockets and do other little things that I now see were inappropriate. After a week or so I could see that I simply wasn't getting their attention like the other staff. They would ignore me and I didn't know what to do. I talked to Amy (my mentor) who helped me sort it out. It was much harder than starting out well and I struggled with establishing my authority for the whole five weeks. I didn't make the same mistake the next time.

Cherri, SCITT trainee

I am a lively person in real life but in class my voice just seemed to shut down. I couldn't seem to keep attention or command the children. My voice was described by a colleague I knew well as 'wimpy'. I was devastated. I did some voice training at the university and on my final school placement I just went for it. I acted the whole time, varying my voice in volume and pitch. Looking back, I feel like I was amplifying my character at the children by using my voice. I suppose that is what you need to do – exaggerate expression and intonation so that all the children in a class are engaged. I still can't believe I was that wimpy. I am still a quiet teacher and keep a quiet class, but my voice and gestures are engaging and not boring.

Ulrika, NQT

I consciously imitated my teacher in my first school. She did 'Heads, fingers, knees and toes' (a sort of action rhyme) to get the attention of the children. I did this too and it helped me establish myself. In my second school I had an older class and used 'OK, listen' because it was the wording the teacher used to get attention. It worked well for me, although the first couple of times I had to wait quite a long time. Now I have my own class I just raise a hand in the air to get attention. It suits the calm sort of ethos I like in class. I think we all find our own style.

Rina, NQT

Dealing with difficult behaviour

You are not the only factor in managing children's behaviour in a classroom. For very young children in the Early Years Foundation Stage, inducting children into what behaviours are and are not acceptable is a major part of the curriculum. Even if you have planned interesting content and presented it well, there will be some children whose behaviour is unacceptable some of the time and in some classes this will represent a significant challenge. You need to learn how to deal with this gradually.

At the start of your school based training you must recognise that you are not alone and seek the support of the teacher. First, you need to watch your teacher carefully to identify whose behaviour is difficult and how the teacher deals with it. Some children will have recognised difficulties with their behaviour that have resulted in action plans to address their needs. In this case they will usually have individual action plans that you need to look at and accommodate in your planning. Some children will also have support from a teaching assistant and behaviour support adviser. You should talk to these people and make sure you know the strategies that they find are working.

When you have identified what the teacher's expectations are, how he or she manages behaviour in class, who finds good behaviour difficult and how the teacher deals with this, you will be starting to teach sessions or lessons. It is important that you take the teacher's role to establish your authority but you do not need to do this unsupported. Ask your teacher to be on hand and discuss what you will do in a number of situations.

If a child acts inappropriately there are a number of ways you can handle the situation.

- **Ignore the inappropriate behaviour – but return to discuss it later, probably in private.**
- **Pass it off without undue emphasis, perhaps saying something like, 'I don't think I caught that ...'. This gives the offender a chance to reconsider.**
- **Act quickly but briefly to administer a routine warning or punishment (such as a name on the board) and move swiftly on to continue what you are doing without making the incident significant.**
- **Assert your authority in one way or another, perhaps by looking shocked or astonished or indicating disapproval. You should only do this where you are not going to generate a conflict you cannot win and are not going to make the whole experience an interesting situation for the child.**
- **Separate the child from the others and deal privately with the issue so that the child is not performing for an audience.**

If you are worried about a particular child or group of children in the class, make sure you are in control of the situation, have considered where they are sitting and with whom and, as you build confidence, ask your teacher to sit with those children or nearby. As your confidence develops you may still want to enlist the teacher to support you by identifying a point at which a child has had enough attention for bad behaviour and will be quietly put into the charge of the teacher. Even when your teacher is not in the class with you, when you are teaching confidently, you should always know where to find him or her (or someone standing in for them) and be able to send two children to get them.

When dealing with poor behaviour it is very important you are assertive in your manner and the way you discuss an incident of bad behaviour.

- **Summarise the behaviour causing the problem in a simple, straightforward manner and do not allow yourself to become emotional: 'I don't like you to twirl around when we are on the mat and you must answer questions when I ask you.'**
- **State how you feel but do not involve other people: 'I am worried about your rudeness and I am sad that you feel you can shout out at me.'**
- **Describe your feelings in simple terms: 'You know our class rule is to be polite to each other at all times. Your shouting makes me feel sad because you know it is not allowed in class.'**
- **Empathise or show sympathy with the other person's view (without endorsing it): 'I understand that not getting a turn makes you feel upset sometimes.'**
- **Specify what you would like the child to do and what you will do: 'I want you to stop saying rude things and twirling around on the mat so that I can offer you a turn. I will make sure I do when I see you sitting quietly.'**
- **Decide what your response to the child's action will be.**

Being assertive and identifying a resolution to a problem is very different from being aggressive or belligerent. You should never lose control of your temper in class. If you do, you may make a situation worse and lose authority with the children. However, it is important to be able to appear cross when necessary.

Frequently asked questions

1. **'I have never taught a class of children, or even more than a small group and I know that I have to take whole classes. Suppose they simply won't do what I ask?'**

If you approach the class correctly, they will do what you ask. Begin your school based training by reading the behaviour policy and observing your teacher. Make absolutely sure you know the whole range of rewards and sanctions so that you can offer these appropriately. Start with a short, carefully planned activity that the children are used to doing, such as reading a story to the class. This will help you to build up your confidence gradually. The most important thing is to appear confident.

2. **'One child in my class is really trying my patience. She interrupts, shouts in class and is openly insolent. Can I send her outside to cool off?'**

First of all you need to read your school policy and talk to your teacher. In general, sending children out of the class is not acceptable, as this might put them at risk. In any case, even thinking of this is very extreme and you should have exhausted the whole range of sanctions before you consider a severe measure such as this. Your school will have a procedure for dealing with poor behaviour, such as writing names on the board, keeping children in for five minutes at play and involving other staff. Explore these with the support of your teacher. Finally, remember that you are not alone on school based training. To re-establish order in the class, you should ask your teacher to work with you in class and help you to manage this child.

3. **'I have a delightful Nursery class. Can I give them sweets to reward good behaviour?'**

It is not really a good idea to reward good behaviour with sweets for a number of reasons. The school will have a health education policy that will certainly not include the use of sweets. It would be a shame to undermine early messages about healthy eating by making sweets a reward. You may also find that some children are allergic to certain ingredients commonly found in sweets, such as lactose or nuts or nut derivatives. Finally, many parents would prefer not to have children associate sweets with rewards and to be in control of the sweets their children eat. Instead of sweets, you can use stickers and praise and take the opportunity of fruit time to enjoy eating together.

4. **'One boy in my class is blatantly rude to me and calls out in my lessons. How should I deal with it?'**

First, discuss this with the teacher. Does he or she have the same problem and what action has he or she taken? You may want to ask your teacher or mentor to observe a lesson so that you can discuss the behaviour that is troubling you. You must decide, preferably with your mentor, exactly what is and is not acceptable. This will stop you over-reacting.

If the school has established practices, such as writing 'strikes' on the board and adding these up to some other punishment, use these. It is always best to use a system known to the child. You should take the child aside, so that he does not have an audience, and discuss clearly and rationally what is acceptable and unacceptable and how you will treat such behaviour. Make sure you find opportunities to praise the child for his efforts at least as often as you have to reprimand him, as this is one way to develop more acceptable behaviour.

5. **'On Friday the class was really difficult and I just lost my temper and went ballistic. Now I feel embarrassed and I am worried about controlling the class.'**

Losing your temper is a sign of desperation and not something you should repeat. You need some support from your mentor or class teacher. Spend a couple of lessons observing how teachers use very small rewards and sanctions (starting with a smile or frown and working up to a sticker or name on a board) before you have a meeting with your mentor. Then review the school policy with the mentor and check you know how to reward and punish in very tiny steps. This is how to keep control of the situation. Are you using time badly, failing to explain tasks or giving children work they cannot do? Discuss this honestly with your mentor and make sure your lessons are well planned with a good pace. This will prevent trouble.

6. **'I am being driven mad by the children in my Year 4 class. Whenever I ask them to do group or individual tasks they constantly ask trivial questions about where to put dates, what to do with rubbers and how to spell words. They don't do it to the teacher.'**

There are two possibilities here. First of all, you may not be explaining the tasks clearly and failing to refer to the support systems the teacher uses. This may have left the children confused. Check you know how your teacher gives instructions and what usual practice is in terms of dates and finding spellings. Enforce these routines politely but firmly and the children will respond to routines they are used to. The second possibility is that the children have noticed that you do not know their routines and are taking advantage of the situation to put off starting work. The answer is the same – show that you know the routines.

REFLECTIVE TASK

Working with your mentor or class teacher (or even another colleague) audit the positive/negative balance of your responses to children.

Start by compiling a list of all the rewards and sanctions you use. For example:

Table 8.1

Rewards	Sanctions
Smile	Ignoring a comment
Eye contact	Frowning at a child
'Well done' (praise)	Asking someone to sit down/be quiet

Your colleagues can use this list to do a tally chart of your rewards/sanctions in a single lesson. Aim to find out:

- **What is the balance of rewards and sanctions in your lesson?**
- **Who do you give most attention to?**
- **What can you do to ensure you give more rewards than sanctions, and that this is a calm sensible reward?**

Child protection

Children and young people have a fundamental right to be protected from harm and have a right to expect schools to provide a safe and secure environment. It is a guiding principle of the law and child protection procedures that the protection and welfare of the child must always be the first priority. The protection of children and young people is a shared community responsibility and failure to provide an effective response can have serious consequences for the child. Teachers and other education staff are in a unique position to identify and help abused children. Your school will have a child protection policy that you should read.

In school based training, if you suspect any child is subject to the categories of abuse identified by the DfE (2014) Keeping Children Safe in Education – neglect, physical injury, sexual abuse or emotional abuse, or a child discloses abuse to you, you must follow the school policy and inform the teacher designated responsible (who will be identified in the school policy). This is a highly confidential matter and you should treat it as such. The teacher responsible may choose to share the information with the class teacher but it is not a matter for you to discuss with other staff.

If a child chooses to disclose abuse to you, you should:

- **listen to them quietly in privacy but do not interrogate them or ask leading questions;**
- **make it clear to the child that you cannot keep the information confidential;**
- **be calm, reassuring and non-judgemental and do not seem to reproach the child, i.e. avoid questions like 'Why didn't you tell … ?'**
- **make a record of what the child has said as soon as you can and date it;**
- **tell the designated teacher for child protection, preferably on the day the disclosure happens, and pass your notes to him or her.**

You can be sure that any allegation of this sort will be dealt with sensitively, swiftly and thoroughly. You may need support yourself to cope with this sort of experience. In the first instance you can get this from your mentor, course tutor or a university counsellor. You can also ring the NSPCC helpline on 0808 800 5000.

A SUMMARY OF KEY POINTS

- On professional school based training you will work with a range of other adults, including other practitioners, teaching assistants, parents, visiting professionals and administrative staff.

- Working closely with other practitioners and teaching assistants involves understanding their roles and planning carefully for their involvement in all parts of the lesson or session.

- Managing the behaviour of the children you are teaching involves signalling clearly that you are the teacher: know what you are doing, have interesting work and high expectations. Sometimes, this is not as simple as it sounds.

- To take the place of the regular teacher you need to know how the school, class and teacher work. Read the school policy, observe the class and the teacher. Make sure that you know the very fine grading of rewards and sanctions and the teacher's expectations for behaviour.

- Act the part of the teacher. Your body language, how you speak to the children and your apparent confidence, together with well-paced lessons and appropriate activities, will work to ensure an orderly learning environment.

- Your teacher is there to support you. As you gain confidence you will take over managing behaviour in class but you should not be afraid to work closely with the teacher to address particular issues.

- Read the school child protection policy and know who the designated teacher responsible is. If you have any child protection concerns, report to the designated teacher and follow it up with a written, dated report.

RESOURCES RESOURCES **RESOURCES** RESOURCES RESOURCES **RESOURCES**

The materials formerly hosted by the DfE as Behaviour 4 Learning are now available at http://www.behaviour2learn.co.uk/about, a website maintained by the University of Northampton.

NSPCC http://www.nspcc.org.uk/helpline: tel 0808 800 5000.

DfE (2014) Keeping Children Safe in Education https://www.gov.uk/government/publications/keeping-children-safe-in-education

There is some very useful advice about working with teaching assistants on the ATL website for new teachers. http://www.new2teaching.org.uk/tzone/education/workingrelationships/TAs.asp

9
Moving on

Learning outcomes

This chapter offers advice about completion of blocks of school based training. By the end of the chapter you will know how to:

- **conclude your time in a particular school;**
- **review your progress on school based training;**
- **prepare for the next block of school based training or your NQT year;**
- **begin to look for a teaching job.**

Concluding a training in a school

The end of a period of training in school is an important time for you. It is a goal you have worked hard to achieve but it is also slightly strange for you to be passing the class back to another teacher. A report of some kind about your assessment will be written by your mentor and/or class teacher and you will discuss with them how well you have achieved your targets. You will also be concluding some important relationships. The first of these is the relationship with your class teacher, who will be used to working closely with you and will have to take up the reins of a class who have become used to you. As your school based training may end before the end of a term, your teacher may need to carry on teaching seamlessly when you leave. In the last week of your school based training you need to make sure you do the following things:

- **Return all the resources you have borrowed. It is very annoying for your teacher to find, a week after you have left, that you have mistakenly retained photocopiable sheets, or computer software.**
- **Check that you have taken all your resources and equipment away, as it will inconvenience everyone if you have to keep coming back.**
- **Mark and record all the work children have done for you. If there are pieces for assessment or Foundation Stage Profile contributions, ensure these are filed in the right place and correctly annotated.**
- **Have a final tidy up and check that all books and resources are in the teacher's allocated places.**
- **Ensure you pass up-to-date records of the work the children have done with you to your teacher. It is a good idea to arrange a time to discuss the records and to highlight the objectives the children have addressed on the medium-term plan. This, with your records, allows the teacher to take over again smoothly.**
- **Check any outstanding commitments. If you have agreed to come back to help with an assembly or a trip, make sure you know the details before you leave. If you are coming back for another placement later, mention this to your teacher.**

Most importantly of all, make sure you thank your teacher explicitly for his or her help and the training they have given you, even if you are coming back to the school or class for a further period of school based training. Make sure you make this more than a casual leave-taking: pick out some specific help they have given you and something you have learned from them. Most trainees follow up thanks with a short note or card. The teacher has given you a great deal of support and entrusted their class to you. It is rewarding for him or her to be reminded that you are grateful for this when they are engaged in the hard work of rebuilding their relationship with the class.

Possibly the most important training relationship you have in school is with your mentor. The formal conclusion to a period of school based training will be a discussion about your progress during the school based training and this will contribute to a report or profile that assesses your performance against the Teachers' Standards. You will look at a draft of your report or the evidence that will contribute to your report. If you are leaving the school, even if you are coming back at a later date, you need to conclude your relationship with your mentor.

- **Return all the resources you have borrowed from your mentor, other staff, the resources room or staffroom.**
- **Check that any displays you are responsible for are complete and labelled.**
- **Check any outstanding commitments and that you have a copy of your report from your mentor.**

Thank your mentor explicitly for the training they have given you. Your mentor may not have taught alongside you every day, like your teacher, but they have made a big contribution to your training. As with your teacher, explicit thanks and a short note are thoughtful gestures.

You may also want to ask your mentor, or head teacher, for a reference. If this is the end of your school based training you may want a reference quite soon (or even during the time you are in school). If this is not the end of your school based training you may still want to have a second or third reference from the mentor or head teacher for a future application for a teaching post. You may also want to ask for references for vacation work or non-teaching posts. When you ask for a reference be explicit.

- **Ask if the mentor or head teacher is prepared to offer you a reference. In most cases a reference is offered gladly. Professionals will not write a bad reference for anyone. They usually simply say they would prefer not to offer a reference. Mentors and head teachers will never decline to offer a reference simply because they do not want the effort.**
- **Who would your mentor prefer to be named – the mentor him or herself or the head teacher?**
- **Check that you know the full name, title and professional position of your mentor or head – it is surprising how often trainees do not get this right.**
- **Say when you expect to be applying for jobs and whether these will be exclusively teaching jobs or will include things like vacation jobs or voluntary work.**
- **Be clear about anything you would like your referee to mention (such as participation in out-of-school events) or avoid mentioning, such as a disability or illness.**
- **Make sure that the mentor or head has your contact details and that you have theirs. You should contact them to let them know when you use their name as a referee in any application.**
- **Always thank your head teacher at the end of a school based training, if you are leaving that school. The head teacher has opened up the school to you and made you welcome.**

Finally, when you finish a period of school based training, you need to conclude your relationship with the class. It will have been a very complex, intense and demanding relationship and leaving the children can make you feel very emotional. The children in your school based training class have played a big part in your training and you will remember some of them for the rest of your career. You have some responsibilities towards them as well. You need to make sure you have returned their work and kept any promises you made to them in terms of rewards such as 'Golden Time', exciting activities or games.

The end of your training time in school is not the time for a sentimental speech, no matter how emotional you feel, but do make sure you explain to the class that you will be leaving them. You should explain this positively so that they understand that this is something you had planned and that you have enjoyed your time with them. Pick out some incidents or lessons you have particularly enjoyed and some examples of good classwork or behaviour. You should also make it clear who will be teaching them now. You might want to put up a poster or card to thank the children for the time you've had as their teacher.

After leaving a school you have a duty of confidentiality towards the school, teachers and children. If you use examples of school documents in assignments, you should ask the permission of the school and make sure that the extract is anonymised. You should not gossip about the schools, the teachers or the children and if you do use examples of your experience or children's work in the professional setting of your course you should do so in such a way that the teachers, school or children involved cannot be identified. This is also important where photos of the school or children have been taken, with the permission of the school.

Reviewing your progress on school based training

You will review your progress as you go through your school based training but there is a key review point towards the end of a block of school based training. There are a number of reasons for this:

- **to check you have done all the tasks you planned and used all the training opportunities on offer;**
- **to review whether you have met targets you set for the school based training or during the school based training;**
- **to identify progress you have made towards demonstrating the Teachers' Standards;**
- **to decide what constitutes evidence of your progress towards the Teachers' Standards and to store this appropriately;**
- **to prepare for a review meeting with your mentor or course tutor;**
- **to prepare a portfolio of work in preparation for a job interview;**
- **to set new targets for future school based trainings, study of particular areas or your NQT year.**

It is important for you to review your targets and progress before the last week of the school based training so that you can identify what progress you have made and the evidence for this. In this way you can be prepared for a meeting with your mentor to discuss your final report. You will be assessed by the mentor and possibly a course tutor but you will have the opportunity to present evidence for your assessment by discussion and referring to your files. You do not have the right to alter their assessment but your mentor will want to make sure your report does justice to your performance against the Teachers' Standards and will consider all the evidence. In this way you can contribute positively to your assessment.

Identifying targets for your NQT year

Your school based training report will summarise your achievements and identify areas for further work. These can be turned into targets for your next school based training or NQT year. All courses of training will have a document you use to guide the process of reflection and review as you complete your initial teacher training and go through your induction year.

Your targets document helps you to:

- **build on your achievements and identify your professional development needs;**
- **make links between your ITT, induction and continuing professional development;**
- **prepare for meetings with your tutors and induction tutor;**
- **set your current priorities in the wider context of career and professional development.**

Your targets help your ITT provider to prepare you to play an active role in your induction period.

The targets should be set with you by your ITT provider near to the end of your training.

As you come to the end of your ITT programme, you will want to think about how far you have come in your professional development. Your ITT provider will also be preparing you for your induction period and helping you to understand your own role in that process.

You should aim to set targets that:

- **reflect and build on the strengths in your practice;**
- **develop aspects of the teacher's role in which you are particularly interested;**
- **provide more experience, or build up your expertise, in areas where you have developed to a more limited extent so far.**

You are not expected to write lengthy reflections. The processes of reflection and professional discussion with your course tutor or mentor are more important and these will be reflected in the notes you make.

- **At this stage, which aspect(s) of teaching do you find most interesting and rewarding?**
- **What has led to your interest in these areas?**
- **How would you like to develop these interests?**
- **As you approach the award of QTS, what do you consider to be your main strengths and achievements as a teacher?**
- **Why do you think this?**
- **What examples do you have of your achievements in these areas?**
- **In which aspects of teaching would you value further experience in the future? For example:**
  - **aspects of teaching about which you feel less confident, or where you have had limited opportunities to gain experience;**
  - **areas of particular strength or interest on which you want to build further.**
- **At the moment, which of these areas do you particularly hope to develop during your induction period?**

As you look ahead to your career in teaching, you may be thinking about your longer term professional aspirations and goals. Do you have any thoughts at this stage about how you would like to see your career develop?

Note down your response to the questions, where you might find evidence to support your thinking, and/or the reasoning that led you to this response. You will want to draw on evidence that is already available, for example:

- **reports on your teaching during your school based training;**
- **observation reports written by your mentor, class teacher or course tutor;**
- **examples of your planning for school based training;**
- **records of targets and objectives set during your ITT programme;**
- **your own audits of your progress towards the Teachers' Standards;**
- **course assignments or subject audits.**

You will want to be able to find this evidence and, if necessary, share it with others, like your tutors. You may wish to copy your notes, to include them in other professional development records or portfolios, or share them with others, for example, to prepare for further discussions with your tutors or mentors. It is for you and your tutor to decide on how evidence can be used in the most supportive way.

Your targets will help to:

- **support your professional development through your NQT year;**
- **support constructive dialogue between NQTs and induction tutors;**
- **make links between induction, continuing professional development and performance management.**

Induction for Newly Qualified Teachers

If you are completing your final placement or towards the end of school based training, you will probably be looking forward to getting a job in teaching and becoming an NQT. Induction for Newly Qualified Teachers is compulsory, follows ITT and is the foundation for continuing professional development throughout your career. The induction period must be undertaken by NQTs who wish to work in maintained schools and non-maintained special schools. The induction period may also be done whilst working in independent schools but not all of them offer this. Check when you apply for jobs, as failure to do a recognised induction may hamper your subsequent teaching career.

During the induction period you have to demonstrate you have continued to meet the Teachers' Standards. You will have an individualised programme of support from a designated induction tutor during your induction year. This includes observation of the your teaching, watching more experienced teachers in different settings, and a professional review of progress at least every half term. You will not teach more than 90 per cent of a normal timetable during the period, to allow your induction to take place.

The head teacher is responsible with appropriate bodies and will make a final recommendation as to whether you have passed or failed your induction period. Appropriate bodies are defined by the DfE as either of:

- **A local authority with which the school reaches agreement**
- **A teaching school (unless you are employed or recommended for QTS by that school)**
- **The National Induction Panel for Teachers (NIPT)**
- **The local authority in which the school is situated (if agreement cannot be reached between the school and one of the above).**

The National College for Teaching and Leadership keeps records of the progress of all teachers through induction and guidance about the process is available at: http://www.education.gov.uk/get-into-teaching/about-teaching/induction-year.

Applying for a teaching job

During your teaching school based training you may start to apply for jobs. This will affect your school based training in a number of ways:

- **you will need time off for visits and interviews;**
- **you will want to use your school based training experience positively in your application;**
- **you will want to ask for references and ensure your referees are clear about what is required.**

Time off for visits and interviews

Jobs are usually advertised by individual schools or NQT pools, a group of schools recruiting together. You must make sure you check the systems in place in your target areas – it is not uncommon for schools to advertise individually and also be part of an education authority pool. When you respond to an advertisement the school, academy chain or education authority will send you an information pack and details of how to apply for the job. Your ITT provider will also give you information.

When you are considering applying for a job you may be invited to look around the school or you may ask to do so. This could present problems because of the time taken out of your school based training, especially if you are applying for a job at some distance from your training school. There is no doubt that an informal visit can be useful to you and some schools schedule specific times to take a large number of applicants around the school together. However, you must consider the impact of absence from school on your training. If you applied for six jobs, visited all the schools and went for interviews at each one, you would miss at least a week of school based training – two weeks if the schools you are applying to are not very close to your school based training school. As you have to complete a certain amount of school based training time in a school and take sustained responsibility for a class on final school based training, a large number of visits could affect the outcome of your school based training. It may be better to try to visit schools after the end of the school day, or to explain to schools that your school based training commitments prevent you from visiting informally. You will almost always be given a tour of the school prior to interview and will have the opportunity to withdraw from the interview after this if you do not think the school would suit you.

If you have applied for a post and are invited to interview, you should ask your mentor for permission to attend: this will involve missing school based training that day. In practice this is a courtesy and you will always be given permission to attend interviews. Mentors and teachers will help you to prepare your application and you should discuss a draft of your letter of application, supporting statement or CV (whatever is requested) with your mentor, if possible. It is also a good idea to ask your mentor or class teacher to help you to prepare for interview. Preparation might take a number of forms:

- **Discussion of hot topics in the educational press or recent initiatives in school is always useful. Discussing these issues with a teacher will help you to explore the issues from another perspective. Consider what the effects of new ideas are for teachers, schools and children.**

- Role playing a mock interview with the mentor, teacher or another member of school staff can help you to conquer nerves and prepare your interview manner. If your course involves a university, you will have access to their careers service and you should use it.
- Asking your teacher to help you to plan any teaching you are required to do as part of your interview. It is not uncommon to be asked to teach something to the class. Although you will not be able to prepare a perfect lesson because you do not know the children, you can still show that you know the relevant curricula, have good ideas, know a range of teaching strategies, are aware of a range of resources and have a good manner with the children. Your teacher or mentor may be able to spot obvious faux pas or overambitious plans if you ask to discuss them.
- If you apply for a job through a teaching pool (for an LA, academy chain or school alliance) you will usually go for an interview for the pool first and may then be invited to look around schools that have jobs available. This is a different sort of school visit from the informal pre-interview visit because you will be looking at a school to see whether you would take a job there. You should go on these visits but be aware of the time you will lose on your school based training.

Using your school based training experience in your application for a teaching post

You should be given support in applying for a teaching post at some point during your ITT programme but it is important that your application includes insights from your school based training because this will show that you have learnt from your experiences.

When you write in response to an advertisement for a teaching post or for details of an NQT pool you will receive a specification for the job (see Figure 9.1). This may be general, like the sample below, or there may be very specific requirements associated with a school. As an NQT, you cannot become a curriculum co-ordinator in your NQT year.

There are two main types of written application for Primary and Early Years teaching posts:

- the LA, school alliance or school application form, which usually includes a personal statement or letter of application;
- your own CV and letter of application.

The information pack you receive from the school, alliance or LA will tell you what is required.

Complete application forms neatly and accurately, in a way that will demonstrate enthusiasm. The usual rules for form filling apply: read the instructions carefully and follow them. Write a draft first (and keep it for future reference); do not leave gaps – write N/A if appropriate; check all your dates and have all your information to hand; make sure your writing is neat and everything is correctly spelled and make sure your personal statement (or letter) is effective. Allow plenty of time to fill in your application – it takes longer than you think – and make sure you have done a thorough review of your school based training and your record of professional development or training plan.

You will be required to write either a supporting statement or letter of application as part of the form or a supporting letter. The first thing you should do to prepare this is to examine thoroughly the specification and/or job description to work out what the school or LA is looking for. Then read the instructions for completing the form very carefully. Filling out this form is a chore but it is your chance to market your skills. Do not be too modest nor make exaggerated claims. You may find the completed form slightly embarrassing, because it spells out your achievements and qualities, but it should not be untruthful.

Newly Qualified Teacher Specification
Experience (Appropriate school based training experience.)
Qualifications (PGCE, QTS, or the ability to achieve this under current DfE regulations.)
Knowledge and aptitudes
Knowledge and understanding of the NC requirements for the relevant age range.
Ability to plan, deliver, monitor and evaluate children's learning
Knowledge and understanding of the principles of assessment and record keeping and their use to promote the educational and personal development of the pupils.
Ability to communicate ideas clearly to a variety of groups.
Understanding of the requirements of children with special educational needs.
Ability to effectively manage and motivate children.
Ability to work as part of a team and to develop positive relationships with pupils, colleagues, parents and where appropriate, outside agencies
Ability to demonstrate a commitment to equality of opportunity for all pupils
Ability to demonstrate a commitment to high educational standards and to maximising the achievement of all pupils.
Ability to demonstrate a commitment to continuing professional development.

Figure 9.1 Sample teaching job specification

There are many ways of writing your letter of application or supporting statement but the following points should be considered.

- **Say why you are applying for this post in particular. Include any local links, faith issues or visits to the school.**
- **Give a brief overview of your training (but do not repeat everything you have put in the application form). Also mention your degree (PGCE or BA/BSc) and any relevant projects or experiences.**
- **Reference to your formal school based trainings including:**
  - **when you did the school based training;**
  - **what years you have taught;**
  - **the level of responsibility you took.**
- **Special features of the school based training such as open plan schools or team teaching.**
- **Examples of how you plan, teach, monitor and evaluate learning outcomes, behaviour management strategies, work with parents, etc.**
- **Write a little about your vision or beliefs for Early Years or Primary education and the principles that underpin your practice. This might be how children learn, classroom management, teaching styles, etc. This gives the school a flavour of what you are like as a teacher.**
- **Details of your personal experiences: leisure interests or involvement with children. Make these relevant to your work as a teacher.**

One of the easier ways to organise this information is to identify a number of subheadings taken from the specification or job description such as:

- **teaching experience (school based training);**
- **commitment to teaching;**
- **knowledge, skills and aptitudes;**
- **planning and organisation;**
- **strengths and interests;**
- **personal qualities.**

Organise your information under these headings. You can then remove your subheadings and have a well organised letter to discuss with your mentor, teacher or careers adviser.

Write a letter of application, of less than two sides of A4, setting out your experience, knowledge, skills and aptitudes and views about education. Discuss this general draft with your mentor or teacher and ask them to tell you about the impact and the impression it makes.

You may find yourself writing a curriculum vitae (CV) for the first time for a job application during your training. Your CV sets out the important information about you, usually on no more than two sides of A4. Make sure you have some good quality, white paper to print on.

If you are basing your CV on a version you have used before, do not just churn it out for job after job. Check first that it matches the specification for each individual job.

PRACTICAL TASK PRACTICAL TASK **PRACTICAL TASK** PRACTICAL TASK **PRACTICAL TASK**

Use the specification in Figure 9.1 to review your experience, qualifications and knowledge, skills and aptitudes. Go through each point asking yourself:

- **What evidence do I have that I meet this criterion?**
- **What have I learned about this on my school based training?**
- **What else do I need to be able to do to achieve this?**

Finally, ask yourself what you want to focus on in your continuing professional development during the induction year.

Things you can leave out of a CV

- There is no need to include your date of birth, age, marital status or ethnic origin.
- A photograph is not necessary for teaching CVs and can trigger subconscious prejudice.
- Do not include your reasons for changing jobs. Keep your CV factual: where you worked and when.
- Do not include failures on your CV. Keep it focused on what you have achieved.
- Do not include salary information.

Things to include on your CV

- Contact details. Make sure that contact details you give will really reach you: if you have an email address that you rarely check, do not include it. Ideally, include your postal address, any telephone numbers you have (landline and mobile) and your email address if you will be checking it frequently.
- Your gender, if it is not obvious from your name.
- A short skills summary or supporting statement (see below).
- Your education. This is best organised as follows: Primary, Secondary, Further, Higher.
- Your qualifications, listed with the most recent first, including results.
- Your work experience and school based training experiences – most recent first (any positions you held more than about ten years ago can be left out).
- Interests – only real and genuine ones, e.g. any sports you actively participate in. If these hobbies and interests can convey a sense of your personality, all the better. Include any non-teaching qualifications that may have arisen from your hobbies or interests here as well.
- Membership of professional associations (not unions).
- Nationality, National Insurance number and referee details (or a sentence to say, 'Referees available on request') can be included at the end of your CV.

A skills summary need only be around 200 words, but you can still cover a lot of ground.

- Write in the first person.
- Every word must be relevant and grammar should be immaculate.
- Use interesting adverbs and adjectives to lift the text.
- Do not just focus on experience. Achievements, accountability and competence are more important.
- Aim to give a sense of your creativity, personal management and integrity: the reader will want to see that you have strong communication skills and are perhaps even leadership material.
- Some people prefer to include a short bulleted list of around six key skills.

Suggested layout

- When designing your CV, you need to be economical with space. While the page should not look cluttered, excess space will look messy and ill thought-out.
- Present your contact details across the top of the first page (like a letterhead) to preserve space.
- Use a clear, standard font such as Times New Roman or Arial.

- Avoid abbreviations unless they are universally understood.
- If you really cannot fit everything on to two sides of A4, try reducing the font size slightly. This will mean the print is still large enough to read, but will give you a little more room to play with. Avoid lines of just one or two words, as this is a waste of space.
- When you have designed your CV on screen, print off a draft version and try to view it through fresh eyes. Is it likely to grab the attention of a reader within a few seconds? Is it visually pleasing? Are there any errors? It is a good idea to ask someone else to cast an eye over it as it is easy to miss typographical errors on documents you have been working on yourself.
- Be aware that this is not a one-off task. Once you have completed your CV, you will need to keep it up to date.

A sample CV is shown in Figure 9.2.

Asking for references

You will usually be asked to supply the names, positions and contact details of two referees. The first should be a senior member of staff of your ITT provider. Check carefully who this should be. It is common for universities to use the name of the head of department, even though your tutor will write the reference. It is essential to get this name right for two reasons. First, if you do not get a first reference from your ITT provider the job advertiser will usually assume you have something to hide. Second, the reference system in a large ITT provider will be geared up to a swift response but it will only work if you get the right name. The wrong name will slow down your reference and may put you at a disadvantage. Your second referee should usually be from your school based training school.

Interview portfolios

As a trainee you will be maintaining a training plan or record of professional development that contains evidence to demonstrate your achievement of the standards. This will contain school based training assessment reports, observation notes, written assignments, mentor meeting notes and other evidence.

You may be asked to take this training plan or record with you to interview. Even if you are not asked to bring a portfolio you may want to do so. You can offer this to your interviewers. They do not have to spend much time looking at it but it does indicate you are well prepared and professional.

An interview portfolio can be a substantial document but, more usually, is a slim document containing some of the following:

- title and content page, preferably with a photo of you teaching happily on it;
- concise CV;
- school based training assessment reports (one or more);
- a really good lesson plan or two, some examples of the work associated with the lesson and the lesson evaluation;
- a mentor, tutor or class teacher observation of a lesson;
- a sample mentor meeting summary;
- an example of a piece of written work (and the marking sheet) if relevant;
- a few photos of you teaching. Choose these carefully as you really want to present a specific image. Generally you might choose one photo of you teaching a large group or class, one of you looking sensitive with a group and, ideally, one of you teaching elsewhere – pond dipping is ideal. Remember, choose photos to suit a particular job. If the school is very IT conscious, make sure there

Emily Jones

529 Highgate Road, Reading, Berkshire RG1 2AB
Telephone: 0128 678 3567, mobile: 07887 987654, e-mail: EMMY00@aol.com

I am a Newly Qualified Teacher trained to teach mathematics to the 3-8 age group. My previous work experience as an accountant in the City enabled me to develop an understanding of management in a large multinational corporation as well as demonstrable communication skills. Part of my role was the delivery of internal training for new staff. During my initial teacher training I taught in an inner-city nursery and the Early Years Foundation Stage unit of a school with a large multi-racial population. In addition to my teaching I developed a successful everyday mathematics after-school workshop for parents that crossed age and race boundaries and was recognised by the head and governors as a constructive addition to the wider school culture.

Education

Primary: 1986–1992 St John's Primary School, Reading
Secondary: 1992–1997 Reading High School for Girls, Reading
Further: 1997–1999 The Abbey Sixth Form College, Wokingham
Higher: 1999–2002 University of Warwick BA
2002–2006 Membership of the Institute of Chartered Accountants
2008–2009 Institute of Education, University of London PGCE

Qualifications

PGCE: Early Years
Degree: mathematics and statistics 2.1
A–levels: mathematics A, statistics A, physics B, general studies B
GCSEs: mathematics A, English literature A, English language B, physics B, history A, ICT A, art B, geography B, French A, biology B

Professional development

During my initial teacher training I completed an LA-run First Aid in the Classroom course and attended a 'Developing Storysacks' training day.

Work Experience

2006–2007 ITT school based trainings: Grove School Nursery, Camden and Nelson Mandela Primary School, Westminster
2002–2006 British International Bank, London, Accountant
1999–2002 Vacation positions with Marks and Spencer and Waterstone's, Reading

Interests

I have run a local Brownies group for some years. I also run to keep fit and have completed the London marathon.

Additional qualifications

Full, clean driving licence.
Berkshire County Junior Football Coaching

Nationality

British

National Insurance Number

TY123456B

Referees available on request

Figure 9.2 Sample CV

is a picture with you using IT. If the school is keen to improve its physical education, a photo of your tag rugby lesson would be ideal. Make sure you follow your school based training school's policy on photograph use and that the school and children are not identifiable.

- One or two photographs of displays, school visits you have been on, after school clubs or assemblies you have done.
- Any evidence of your special interest – coaching certificates, first aid, cookery, etc.

In practice, trainees tell us that interview panels do not spend much time on interview portfolios and usually just flick through the content. However, by preparing this you not only demonstrate professionalism but also have the chance to present a tailored image of your achievements to the panel in addition to your written application.

RESODURCES RESOURCES RESOURCES RESOURCES RESOURCES RESOURCES

Detailed guidance about induction is now available at http://www.education.gov.uk/get-into-teaching/about-teaching/induction-year.

The statutory requirements for induction can be found at: https://www.gov.uk/government/uploads/system/uploads/attachment_data/file/375304/Statutory_induction_for_newly_qualified_teachers_guidance_revised_October_2014.pdf

(It is simpler to go to https://www.gov.uk/ and then search for 'induction'.)

Detailed information about applying for a teaching post, and how to manage the interview process is available from the Association of Graduate Careers Advisory Services (AGCAS) Target Jobs site at: http://targetjobs.co.uk/career-sectors/teaching-and-education

Most school vacancies are advertised in the *Times Educational Supplement* (Fridays) – www.tes-jobs.co.uk

The Guardian (Tuesdays) – www.jobsunlimited.co.uk.

The Daily Telegraph (Independent Schools) – www.telegraph.co.uk.

The Independent (Thursdays) – www.independent.co.uk.

Some of these operate an electronic job alert system.

For information about teaching in the private sector:

Incorporated Association of Preparatory Schools (IAPS) at: https://iaps.uk/

Your union is an excellent source of help, advice and support in applying for a teaching post:

www.teachersunion.org.uk (NASUWT).

www.data.teachers.org.uk (NUT).

www.askatl.org.uk (ATL).

Other useful online resources for finding a teaching post are available at:

www.eteach.com.

www.prospects.ac.uk.

Make sure you also use your local or university careers service.

Glossary

Academy schools are state funded schools in England which are directly funded by central government (specifically, the Department for Education) and independent of direct control by the local authority.

Academy chain An academy chain is a partnership between a group of academies. Chains vary in size and composition. Some are loose, informal collaborations. Others have a more formal structure and some are large nationwide chains such as Oasis, E-ACT and United Learning.

ATL Association of Teachers and Lecturers. For further details see www.askatl.org.uk/

ATP Approved Training Provider. For further details see www.dfes.gov.uk/providersregister/

BA with QTS Bachelor of arts with qualified teacher status. A degree in an arts or humanities-based subject which also leads to qualified teacher status.

BEd with QTS Bachelor of education with qualified teacher status. A degree in education which also leads to qualified teacher status.

BSc with QTS Bachelor of science with qualified teacher status. A degree in a science-based subject which also leads to qualified teacher status.

Class teacher A teacher of the class with which you do most of your work during a placement.

CPD Continuing professional development. Your initial training can only take you so far in teaching. To develop and progress, you will need further professional development experience, which may range from completing a Masters degree to attending a short course after school.

DfE Department for Education. The English government department which creates policy. For further details see https://www.gov.uk/government/organisations/department-for-education

EAL English as an additional language.

Extended school A school that provides a range of services and activities often beyond the school day to help meet the needs of its pupils, their families and the wider community.

Foundation stage The earliest years of schooling for UK children (ages 3–5 years).

Free school. A non-profit-making, independent, state-funded school which is free to attend but which is not controlled by a Local Authority. Free schools may be set up by parents, education charities and religious groups.

HEI Higher education institution. A university, school or college offering degree-level and postgraduate education.

Humanities A collective term for a range of subjects including: history, geography, religious studies, sociology and others.

ICT Information and communications technology. This term is no longer used in reference to a National Curriculum subject, having been replaced in 2013 by 'Computing'.

Induction period Following recommendation for the award of QTS you are required to undertake a successful period of induction. For more information see https://www.gov.uk/government/publications/induction-for-newly-qualified-teachers-nqts

Inset In-service education and training. Training for qualified teachers.

ITT Initial teacher training. Course of training that leads to qualified teacher status (QTS).

ITT provider A school, college or university that offers initial teacher training courses.

Key Stages The different stages of compulsory schooling in the UK. The teacher training you receive will be provided according to the needs of the key stages you intend to teach. If you are training to teach Primary or Early Years, you will usually train for two key stages, but need to know about those above and below. Some courses will train teachers for KS2 and KS3, crossing the usual age at which children move between primary and secondary schools.

- **Foundation Key Stage Children aged 3–5 or EYFS Children aged birth to 5.**
- **KS1 Key Stage 1. First stage of compulsory schooling for UK children (ages 5–7 years).**
- **KS2 Key Stage 2. Second stage of compulsory schooling for UK children (ages 7–11 years).**
- **KS3 Key Stage 3. Third stage of compulsory schooling for UK children (ages 12–13 years).**
- **KS4 Key Stage 4. Fourth stage of compulsory schooling for UK children (ages 14–16 years).**

LA Local authority. These organisations (counties, boroughs) provide services for schools in their area.

LSA Learning support assistant.

Maintained school A school that is maintained by the state.

Mentor The person in school who manages your placement offering advice, support and, usually, assessing your progress. The details of the role of your mentor will be in your course information.

MFL Modern foreign languages. French, Spanish, German, Gujarati, etc. MFL for all primary pupils is now a compulsory part of the National Curriculum.

Middle school A middle school has pupils from KS2 and KS3. Depending on the age balance of those pupils the school can be deemed primary or secondary.

MPS Main Pay Scale. Determines classroom teachers' basic salaries. There are now two scales: one for England and Wales and one for inner London. For further details consult your union.

NASUWT National Union of Schoolmasters Union of Women Teachers. For further details see www.nasuwt.org.uk/

NC National Curriculum. Covers what pupils should be taught in state-maintained schools. The National Curriculum embraces 12 subjects overall, and is divided into four key stages according to age. Details are available online at: https://www.gov.uk/government/collections/national-curriculum

NQT Newly qualified teacher. A teacher who has just been recommended for qualified teacher status and who needs to complete an induction period to confirm the award.

NUT National Union of Teachers. For more information, see www.teachers.org.uk/

Ofsted Office for Standards in Education The body responsible for inspection in schools and teacher training. See www.ofsted.gov.uk/

OTTP Overseas trained teacher programme. An individually tailored programme of training and assessment enabling OTTs to achieve qualified teacher status in England. For more information, see https://www.gov.uk/qualified-teacher-status-qts

PE Physical education.

PGCE Postgraduate Certificate of Education. A teacher training qualification which may be at Postgraduate (Master's) level or at Undergraduate (H) level, in which case it may be referred to as a Professional Certificate.

Profile report This is the document completed at the end of your placement which sets out your progress towards meeting the Teachers' Standards and your targets for future work. It may have another name (report, assessment, etc.). It will form part of your training record.

PSHE Personal, social and health education.

PTA Parent-teacher association. For general information see http://www.pta.org.uk/

QTS Qualified Teacher Status. The status trainee teachers achieve. Recommendation for this is achieved by meeting all of the required Teachers' Standards. It is confirmed after a period of induction. You must have this qualification to teach in a state-maintained school.

SCITT School-centred initial teacher training. Teacher training provided by schools, sometimes in partnership with higher education institutions and local education authorities.

School Direct A school-led training course in which you learn 'on the job' in a school. These courses may be run by individual schools or a group of schools working together. See: http://www.education.gov.uk/get-into-teaching/teacher-training-options/school-based-training

Schools in special measures Schools deemed by Her Majesty's Chief Inspector of Schools to be failing to provide an acceptable standard of education for their pupils.

SEN Special educational needs. For some information see https://www.gov.uk/children-with-special-educational-needs/overview

SENCO SEN coordinator. The teacher in school with responsibility for the delivery of services for children with special educational needs.

TA Teaching assistant.

Teachers' Standards These are the standards you have to achieve to be recommended for the award of QTS at the end of your ITT. See https://www.gov.uk/government/publications/teachers-standards

Teaching school Teaching schools are outstanding schools that work with others to provide high-quality training and development for new and experienced school staff. A teaching school will have a strong track record of collaborative working and play a key role in the leadership of a teaching school alliance.

Teaching school alliance A group of schools and other partners that commit to working collaboratively supported by one or more teaching schools. They may be cross phase and cross sector, working across local authorities and include different types of organisations. The strategic partners may be schools, universities and others.

TES *Times Educational Supplement*. A good source of information about teaching job vacancies. See www.tes.co.uk/

Training record or training plan This is a document which summarises your progress towards the standards for QTS and the targets you still need to meet. It usually starts with information about your experience and skills before ITT and is created by adding information about your progress, such as audits of subject knowledge, assignment feed- back, placement profiles, etc. The final document will be your Induction Profile, which sets out your training targets for the Induction period.

Voluntary aided schools Schools in England and Wales, maintained by the LA, for which a foundation (generally religious) appoints most of the governing body.

Voluntary controlled schools Schools in England and Wales, maintained by the LA, for which a foundation (generally religious) appoints some – but not most – of the governing body.

Year 1 to Year 13 The way year groups are divided in English schools, from nursery through to sixth form:

- **Reception year: 4/5-year-olds;**
- **Year 1: 5/6-year-olds;**
- **Year 2: 6/7-year-olds;**
- **Year 3: 7/8-year-olds;**
- **Year 4: 8/9-year-olds;**
- **Year 5: 9/10-year-olds;**
- **Year 6: 10/11-year-olds;**
- **Year 7: 11/12-year-olds**
- **Year 8: 12/13-year-olds;**
- **Year 9: 13/14-year-olds;**
- **Year 10: 14/15-year-olds;**
- **Year 11: 15/16-year-olds;**
- **Year 12: 16/17-year-olds;**
- **Year 13: 17/18-year-olds.**

Index